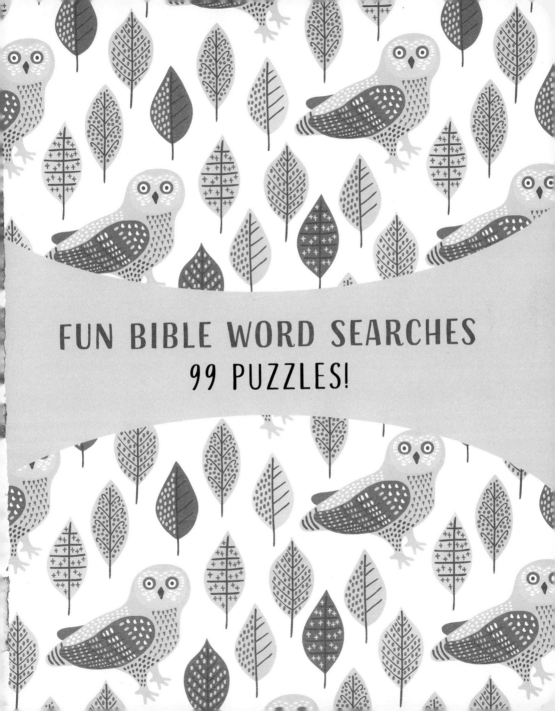

# FUN BIBLE WORD SEARCHES
## 99 PUZZLES!

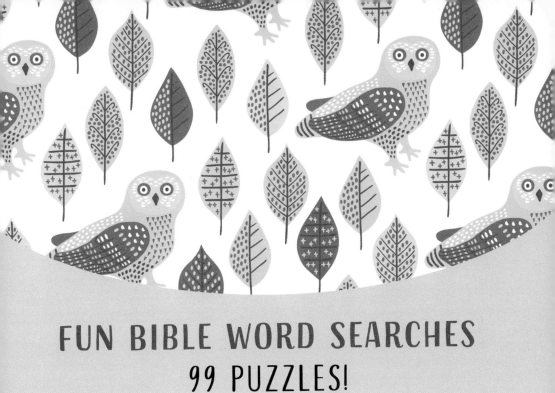

# FUN BIBLE WORD SEARCHES
## 99 PUZZLES!

BARBOUR BOOKS
An Imprint of Barbour Publishing, Inc.

ISBN 978-1-64352-093-3

Puzzles designed by Ashley Schrock, Brigitta Nortker, Kelly McIntosh, Laurie Muckley, Rebecca Germany, and Shalyn Sattler.

All scripture quotations are taken from the King James Version of the Bible.

Published by Barbour Books, an imprint of Barbour Publishing, Inc., 1810 Barbour Drive, Uhrichsville, Ohio 44683, www.barbourbooks.com

*Our mission is to inspire the world with the life-changing message of the Bible.*

 Member of the
Evangelical Christian
Publishers Association

Printed in China.

# WELCOME TO
# FUN BIBLE WORD SEARCHES!

If you like Bible word searches, you'll love this book. Here are 99 puzzles to expand your Bible knowledge and test your word search skills, as thousands of search words—each one selected from the King James Version of the Bible—await your discovery. You're in for hours of fun!

*Fun Bible Word Searches* contains several types of puzzles. You'll find traditional word search lists, with 18–35 entries based on a common theme, as well as scripture passages with the search words printed in **bold type**. When a phrase is **bold and underlined**, those words will be found together in the puzzle grid. Some search lists will include only scripture references for passages relating to a common theme. In these cases, you won't be looking for a word but the actual scripture number in the grid. Keep your eyes and pencils sharp. You can *count* on these puzzles to be especially challenging.

You'll also find a few "secret message word searches"—after you've found all of the hidden words, read the leftover, uncircled letters starting in the upper left-hand corner. As you go from left to right and then down the page, line by line, you'll find a secret trivia question to test your Bible knowledge!

Also included are two new types of puzzles: "crooked" and "crossover" searches. In the first type, crooked puzzles, the words you are searching for will not appear in a straight line but will bend at an angle, providing you with even more of a challenge! The crossover puzzles feature hidden words, each of which have a partner word that crosses it. So, once you have found the first word, keep your eyes peeled for its intersecting partner!

Finally, you'll find a few "one word" puzzles. . .these puzzles feature a single search word—such as "miracle" or "Jerusalem"—and you'll have to find it a specified number of times in the puzzle grid. It's tougher than you might guess. . .

Of course, answers are provided, appearing at the back of the book.

There's not much else to say, other than this: Enjoy!

# one

# THE COMING OF THE LORD

Be **patient** therefore, **brethren**, unto the coming of the **Lord**. Behold, the **husbandman** waiteth for the **precious fruit** of the **earth**, and hath long patience for it, until he receive the **early** and **latter rain**. Be ye also patient; stablish your **hearts**: for the **coming** of the Lord **draweth nigh**. **Grudge** not one against another, brethren, lest ye be **condemned**: behold, the **judge standeth** before the **door**. Take, my brethren, the **prophets**, who have **spoken** in the **name** of the Lord, for an **example of suffering affliction**, and of **patience**.

JAMES 5:7–10

# WORD SEARCH

```
N E R H T E R B Y P L O B H B
L E E X A M P L E A L T U C S
O A D F H T R A E A N S J O T
R E R R D A M A N E B U K M E
S P O K E N R P I A D F O I H
U R L D N B R T N G M F P N P
O L O O M U A D E I N E S S O
I A P O E P M C T I U R F T R
C T R H D A L E C N E I T A P
E T E C N E F M O F A N S N S
R E C H O X F A M N I G H D T
P R I R C S A X I B S U H E R
D R A W E T H E N L R A E T A
R I A E G D U R G G D U J H E
N A F F L I C T I O N F U S H
```

# 2

## BAPTIZE

In this puzzle, can you find the word **baptize** 26 different times? It may help to make a tally mark in the space below each time you find one.

John answered, saying unto them all, I indeed baptize you with water; but one mightier than I cometh, the latchet of whose shoes I am not worthy to unloose: he shall baptize you with the Holy Ghost and with fire.

LUKE 3:16

# WORD SEARCH

```
B  A  P  T  I  Z  E  P  A  I  B  Z  E  E  P
A  Z  I  E  B  E  Z  I  T  P  A  B  Z  A  B
P  I  B  A  P  T  I  Z  E  A  P  I  I  T  A
T  E  A  B  A  P  T  I  Z  E  T  Z  T  E  P
I  B  P  A  Z  E  P  E  T  P  I  E  P  B  T
Z  E  T  P  E  I  A  Z  A  T  Z  P  A  A  I
E  Z  I  T  P  A  B  B  B  I  E  T  B  P  Z
T  I  Z  I  A  B  T  A  T  A  Z  A  A  T  E
E  T  E  Z  E  P  E  P  P  E  P  Z  P  I  P
Z  P  A  E  Z  Z  A  E  Z  T  B  T  T  Z  T
I  A  P  A  I  B  Z  I  I  P  I  A  I  E  A
T  B  Z  T  T  A  T  Z  A  T  B  Z  Z  Z  P
P  I  P  I  P  P  E  A  Z  B  P  A  E  E  E
A  A  Z  E  A  E  Z  I  T  P  A  B  I  A  T
B  I  T  B  B  A  P  T  I  Z  E  A  B  Z  P
```

## 3

*three*

# ASK AND BELIEVE

If any of you **lack wisdom**, let him **ask of God**, that **giveth** to all **men liberally**, and **upbraideth** not; and it shall be **given** him. But let him ask in **faith**, **nothing** wavering. For he that wavereth is like a **wave** of the **sea** driven with the **wind** and **tossed**. For let not that **man** think that he shall **receive** any thing of the Lord. A **double minded** man is **unstable** in all his **ways**.

JAMES 1:5–8

# WORD SEARCH

```
A T T U E L B U O D C K L T R
N O H T I A F I C G R E C A S
E S E L B A T S N U N T S O C
R S L A C K R O E S T K E A L
P E I N M A T Y V H O Y W N G
W D E V P H R N I F G F O R Y
I M W S I D O M G I D U N S L
M O I N S T A O B N L E G I L
I M G E N G D V I E T G T O A
N U M O D S I W S K S I H A R
D R E C E I V E M N O V S T E
E E V A W N A T H I N E Y G B
D F A I T E M C R L O T A M I
M I U P B R A I D E T H W E L
U N S T M I N D T H I G T R A
```

# ADJECTIVES FOR GOD

**Almighty** (Ezekiel 10:5)

**Blessed** (1 Timothy 1:11)

**Eternal** (Deuteronomy 33:27)

**Everlasting** (Isaiah 40:28)

**Faithful** (Deuteronomy 7:9)

**Gracious** and **Merciful** (Nehemiah 9:31)

**Great** and **Terrible** (Nehemiah 1:5; modern translations say "great and awesome")

**Holy** (Joshua 24:19)

**Invisible** (Colossians 1:15)

**Jealous** (Exodus 20:5)

**Living** (Joshua 3:10)

**Mighty** (Isaiah 9:6)

**Most high** (Genesis 14:18)

**One** (Mark 12:32)

**Righteous** (Psalm 7:9)

**True** (2 Chronicles 15:3)

**Uncorruptible** (Romans 1:23)

**Unknown** (Acts 17:23)

**Wise** (1 Timothy 1:17)

# WORD SEARCH

```
E R E V E R L A S T I N G X Z
L F I K E M I G H T Y T O N A
B L A G R E A J R N S E L D E
I B U I H I H E H A C R Y L T
T E L S T T G A E L C R B S E
P C T E A H E L B I S I V N I
U I U E S O F O E A T B O L W
R W R R R E T U U P Y L M U B
R G E I M N R S L S T E O F S
O N L A H T A R N A H S S I O
C I W I S E R L K I G S T C D
N V H H C O L Y N H I E H R J
U I O A C S L U O U M D I E E
E L T N J T O K W M L B G M Y
Y I U N K N O W N S A N H O L
```

# *five*

## PROMISE THROUGH FAITH

For the **promise**, that he should be the **heir** of the **world**, was not to **Abraham**, or to his seed, through the **law**, but through the **righteousness** of **faith**. For if they which are of the law be heirs, faith is <u>**made void**</u>, and the promise made of none effect: because the law worketh **wrath**: for where no law is, there is no **transgression**. Therefore it is of faith, that it might be by **grace**; <u>**to the end**</u> the promise might be **sure** to all the **seed**; not to that only which is of the law, but to that also which is of the faith of Abraham; who is the **father** of us all, (As it is written, I have made thee a father of <u>**many nations**</u>,) before him whom he **believed**, even **God**, who quickeneth the **dead**, and calleth <u>**those things**</u> which be not as though they were.

ROMANS 4:13–17

# WORD SEARCH

```
A C T H O S E T H I N G S B J
M G S S E N S U O E T H G I R
A T R A N S G R E S S I O N I
N N K N G N B E L I E V E D E
Y D N Y C S S M P L G T D F H
N C B G T I Q U D D D N W A L
A N Z C M B B A R A R D R V N
T D E O B S A E E E N B A G O
I G R A C E M D N E E H T O T
O P X C N A N R G M M K H D L
N D E F H N E A E N R D Y J M
S O F A T H E R X C D E M N B
J K R I E S D D I O V E D A M
D B B T G R Y I O I N S V G B
A C N H V D E T Q E D L R O W
```

# COUPLES CROSS

*In this puzzle, you will be given the name of a man; you must find his wife. Your search will be aided by the fact that the husband's and wife's names cross over each other in the puzzle.*

**Abraham** and _____
(Genesis 20:2)

**Adam** and _____
(Genesis 3:20)

**Ananias** and _____
(Acts 5:1)

**Aquila** and _____
(Acts 18:2)

**Boaz** and _____
(Ruth 4:13)

**David** and _____
(2 Samuel 12:24)

**Hosea** and _____
(Hosea 1:3)

**Isaac** and _____
(Genesis 24:67)

**Jacob** and _____
(Genesis 29:28)

**Joseph** and _____
(Matthew 1:20)

**Moses** and _____
(Exodus 2:21)

**Zacharias** and _____
(Luke 1:13)

# WORD SEARCH

```
A X B U R M R N W J P A D T Y
Z E L T A E L E H K O L N R H
C M S H M B K A B G Q S A M L
P N V O P R R D Z E R M E C J
U R G A H A U A F P K W A P N
S Y I P S L O T H R N A D G H
Z T J S E B P A H A S N H U A
R A K H C N L T W I M A Q B K
B O C A J I E D M S R F E A P
A A Y H U B L J A O Z H R N L
R D E Q A F H L P V S P G A I
S V A S D R T P A H I E H N O
E H I M X U I Y T E W D S I U
P L W G R Z N A R I H P P A S
E Y U E P T B U S D T G R S F
```

# seven

# A DOER OF THE WORD

But be ye **doers** of the **word**, and not **hearers** only, **deceiving** your own **selves**. For if any be a hearer of the word, and not a doer, he is like unto a **man beholding** his **natural face** in a **glass**: for he **beholdeth himself**, and **goeth** his **way**, and **straightway forgetteth** what **manner** of man he was. But whoso **looketh** into the **perfect law** of **liberty**, and **continueth** therein, he being not a forgetful hearer, but a doer of the **work**, this man shall be **blessed** in his **deed**.

JAMES 1:22–25

# WORD SEARCH

```
D O H T E O G L O H E B H A M
G W D E C E N G L A R U T A N
O O C O N T I N U E T H E L S
N R Y G L A D F W O R K D B T
A D T W A F L S A M S S L L R
M S R N F E O A D W S H O E A
L M E A S L H O W O A E H S I
O I B M B A E W S E L V E S G
O H I D E R B L G R G A B E H
K H L S S O L O O K E T H D T
E B E H H T E T T E G R O F W
Y D T C E F R E P D E C A F A
X R E N N A M A M E W A N E Y
D E C E I V I N G A V L E S H
W O R P D B I L Y N I T N O C
```

# GOD MEANT IT FOR GOOD

When Joseph's **brethren** saw that their **father** was dead, they said, **Joseph** will **peradventure** hate us, and will certainly **requite** us all the **evil** which we did unto him. And they sent a **messenger** unto Joseph, saying, Thy father did **command** before he died, **saying**, So shall ye say unto Joseph, **Forgive**, <u>I pray thee</u> now, the **trespass** of thy brethren, and <u>their sin</u>; for they did unto thee evil: and now, we pray thee, forgive the trespass of the **servants** of the God of thy father. And Joseph **wept** when <u>they spake</u> unto him. And his brethren also went and <u>fell down</u> **before** his **face**; and they said, **Behold**, we be thy servants. And Joseph said unto them, <u>**Fear not**</u>: for am I in the <u>**place of God**</u>? But as for you, ye **thought** evil against me; but God **meant** it unto **good**, to <u>**bring to pass**</u>, as it is this day, to **save** much **people alive**.

Genesis 50:15–20

*Secret message:*

\_\_\_\_\_ \_\_\_\_\_ \_\_\_\_\_ _____ \_\_\_\_\_ _____

\_\_\_\_\_ _____ _____ _____?

# WORD SEARCH

```
P  E  O  P  L  E  J  O  S  E  P  H  F  W  H
E  C  A  F  S  O  W  A  S  T  L  H  E  S  E
R  F  A  A  T  S  G  N  I  Y  A  S  A  E  H
A  E  T  T  D  N  A  M  M  O  C  V  R  R  N
D  T  T  H  E  Y  S  P  A  K  E  R  N  V  W
V  H  B  E  O  O  W  F  O  E  O  M  O  A  O
E  E  J  R  O  U  S  E  H  T  F  E  T  N  D
N  I  V  E  E  P  G  T  P  H  G  A  A  T  L
T  R  R  I  N  T  Y  H  D  T  O  N  H  S  L
U  S  E  I  G  A  H  S  T  E  D  T  I  D  E
R  I  Q  L  R  R  L  R  E  V  E  D  L  R  F
E  N  U  P  N  F  O  I  E  E  A  O  R  F  B
E  V  I  L  U  L  B  F  V  N  H  O  R  O  T
H  E  T  R  S  M  E  S  S  E  N  G  E  R  X
T  R  E  S  P  A  S  S  B  E  F  O  R  E  X
```

# NINE

# NEHEMIAH PRAYS FOR ISRAEL

And said, I **beseech** thee, O LORD **God of heaven**, the great and terrible God, that keepeth **covenant** and **mercy** for them that love him and observe his commandments: Let thine **ear** now be attentive, and thine **eyes** open, that thou mayest hear the prayer of **thy servant**, which I pray before thee now, day and night, for the **children** of **Israel** thy servants, and **confess** the sins of the children of Israel, which we have **sinned** against thee: both I and my father's **house** have sinned. We have dealt very corruptly against thee, and have not kept the commandments, nor the **statutes**, nor the judgments, which thou commandedst thy servant **Moses**. Remember, I beseech thee, the word that thou commandedst thy servant Moses, saying, If ye transgress, I will **scatter** you abroad among **the nations**: But if ye turn unto me, and keep my commandments, and do them; though there were of you cast out unto the **uttermost** part of the heaven, yet will I **gather** them from thence, and will bring them unto the place that I have **chosen** to set my name there.

Now these are thy servants and thy people, whom thou hast **redeemed** by thy great power, and by thy strong **hand**. O LORD, I beseech thee, let now thine ear be **attentive** to the **prayer** of thy servant, and to the prayer of thy servants, who desire to fear thy name: and **prosper**, I pray thee, thy servant this day, and grant him mercy in the sight of this **man**.

NEHEMIAH 1:5–11

# WORD SEARCH

```
H S A R T Y B O P R A Y E R E
A O S N E V A E H F O D O G M
J S U E K M A M S U Q E X A I
R I F S F R O E P E M N C T H
E N E S E N B S Y H E S S H C
T N A N E V O C E E H C T E D
T E X O R I R C S S N H R E
A D W I X E S H T F H E Y R M
C H E T M Z A O A E E R S E E
S D W A D O U S T O N D E P E
Q U I N S O C E U B A L R S D
P H A E L E K N T X M I V O E
M H L H T I S S E I G H A R R
U U T T E R M O S T O C N P P
L E A R S I E V I T N E T T A
```

# 10
## ELI'S FALL

And the man said unto **Eli**, I am he that came out of the **army**, and I **fled** to day out of the army. And he said, What is there done, my son? And the **messenger** answered and said, **Israel** is fled before the **Philistines**, and there hath been also a <u>**great slaughter**</u> among the people, and <u>**thy two sons**</u> also, **Hophni** and **Phinehas**, are dead, and the <u>**ark of God**</u> is taken. And it came to pass, when he made mention of the ark of God, that he **fell** from off the seat **backward** by the side of the **gate**, and his **neck brake**, and he died: for he was an <u>**old man**</u>, and **heavy**. And he had **judged** Israel **forty years**.

1 SAMUEL 4:16–18

# WORD SEARCH

```
S M A P P L E D O G F O K R A
N E K I W I L O R A N G E G Z
O S N P I T E P I Z Z G N R S
S S Q I N M A X C V B L L E F
O E Y V T B R D R A W K C A B
W N E T H S S M K D L R E T I
T G A O R L I V E W E Z K S P
Y E R A Q O N L Y L F P O L O
H R S Z K P F J I P K G L A I
T S E R C T Y L N H T U D U U
B R A K E V B N O E P L M G Y
S A H E N I H P A A T R A H T
H J K L O I H P Z V Y T N T R
G F D S A N B N M Y E A S E E
N I C E I J U D G E D Y M R A
```

# LINEAGE OF NOAH

This is the **book** of the **generations** of Adam. In the day that **God** created **man**, in the <u>**likeness of God**</u> made he him; <u>**male and female**</u> created he them; and **blessed** them, and called their name Adam, in the **day** when they were **created**.

GENESIS 5:1–2

| | |
|---|---|
| **Adam** | **Jared** |
| **Seth** | **Enoch** |
| **Enos** | **Methuselah** |
| **Cainan** | **Lamech** |
| **Mahalaleel** | **Noah** |

SEE GENESIS 5:1–32

# WORD SEARCH

```
S  E  S  B  K  E  X  I  M  N  H  G  Z  O  T
N  N  F  O  Y  A  W  L  O  E  T  D  H  Y  A
I  U  O  O  N  U  T  A  U  K  E  Y  S  D  D
K  B  U  I  U  E  H  S  I  T  S  U  O  O  E
D  L  N  R  T  N  U  B  A  O  H  G  A  G  R
H  B  A  E  R  A  L  E  Y  A  D  T  U  F  A
A  L  W  M  D  O  R  O  B  A  L  D  E  O  J
L  O  O  A  E  C  U  E  Y  L  S  E  K  S  O
E  G  M  G  E  C  V  Y  N  I  B  S  O  S  E
S  I  U  S  O  Y  H  A  T  E  Z  S  O  E  W
U  H  E  A  R  D  M  C  O  U  G  E  L  N  U
H  T  M  A  H  A  L  A  L  E  E  L  L  E  P
T  A  H  C  O  N  E  Q  U  I  N  B  O  K  E
E  L  A  M  E  F  D  N  A  E  L  A  M  I  R
M  E  E  T  U  P  N  N  A  N  I  A  C  L  A
```

# OBEY YOUR MASTERS

**Servants**, **obey** in all things your **masters** according to the **flesh**; not with **eyeservice**, as **menpleasers**; but in singleness of heart, <u>**fearing God**</u>; and **whatsoever** ye do, do it **heartily**, as to the Lord, and not <u>**unto men**</u>; knowing that of the Lord ye **shall** receive the **reward** of the **inheritance**; for ye <u>**serve the Lord**</u> Christ. But he that doeth **wrong** shall **receive** for the wrong which he <u>**hath done**</u>: and there is no **respect** of **persons**.

Colossians 3:22–25

# WORD SEARCH

```
S L A Y L I T R A E H Y T E R
N R I O B E Y N T O M E V N Y
O T C E P S E R L A F I C K O
S S R E S A E L P N E M E L D
R E L O V W Y I G C A P C S R
E R C H A Z E B E A R Q N R O
P V G R O U S R N D I U A E L
N A D E L K E A O T N A T T E
E N I W L Y R W H E G N I S H
M T H A A K V Y O U G E R A T
O S E I H E I F T A O N E M E
T H C P S B C A L K D R H I V
N G N O R W E C H E A K N C R
U H A T H D O N E O S R I P E
L E M R E V E O S T A H W O S
```

# A CROOKED CHOICE

*Sin has a way of putting a crook in our lives. But we can't allow sins—concealed or revealed—to trip us up. In this puzzle, each hidden word will bend at an angle instead of appearing in one straight line.*

**Adultery** (Exodus 20:14)

**Blasphemy** (Matthew 12:31)

**Boasting** (James 4:16)

**Covet** (Exodus 20:17)

**Cursing** (Psalm 59:12)

**Deceit** (Job 27:4)

**Disobedience** (Ephesians 5:6)

**Divisions** (Romans 16:17)

**Drunkenness** (Romans 13:13)

**Envy** (Proverbs 14:30)

**False witness** (Exodus 20:16)

**Fornication** (Galatians 5:19)

**Hatred** (Proverbs 10:12)

**Hypocrisy** (Isaiah 32:6)

**Idolatry** (1 Samuel 15:23)

**Jealousy** (Proverbs 6:34)

**Lasciviousness** (Ephesians 4:19)

**Lying** (Psalm 120:2)

**Murder** (Jeremiah 7:9)

**Pride** (Proverbs 8:13)

**Rebellion** (Deuteronomy 31:27)

**Slander** (Proverbs 10:18)

**Strife** (1 Corinthians 3:3)

**Witchcraft** (1 Samuel 15:23)

# WORD SEARCH

```
B E R G I V R E D L S E D I H
E E W P O S E M L N A Y Z R D
B D L C N B N T Y D A S H P E
O C I L S O L O I N G L C A R
S E E E I T I A I R E N S I T
I D R I N O R T S S I V I D V
D U R D T C N I A P H E M Y I
M Y S U E A E S F C L K A S O
K S I P C R S A E I R E L S U
A I N B H E L G Y N J V O E S
F R G Y N T U W R R Y N U N N
A C P T E G D I T O D E S N E
L O I R O N A T A F W R Y E S
S W Y H C I R C L O D I U K S
E B O A S T Q H C R A F T N X
```

# GRACE BE UNTO YOU

**Elect** according to the **foreknowledge** of **God** the **Father**, through **sanctification** of the **Spirit**, unto **obedience** and **sprinkling** of the **blood** of <u>**Jesus Christ**</u>: **Grace** unto you, and **peace**, be multiplied. Blessed be the God and Father of our **Lord** Jesus Christ, which according to his abundant **mercy** hath begotten us again unto a **lively hope** by the **resurrection** of Jesus Christ from the **dead**, to an **inheritance incorruptible**, and **undefiled**, and that **fadeth** not away, reserved in **heaven** for you, who are kept by the **power** of God through **faith** unto **salvation** ready to be **revealed** in the last time.

1 PETER 1:2–5

# WORD SEARCH

```
F P E C A R G G Y H E A V E N
N O F A T H E R C D V A E R P
O C R R E S U R R E C T I O N
I S E E L O R D E C A D W B L
T P C V K P E S M N E E M E I
A I A E D N P O H A R Q E D D
C R E A O D O G D T A S R I E
I I P L O B H W B I I B C E L
F T C E L E S P L R E A F N I
I F O D B E L H T E D A F C F
T P O Y L E V I L H D S L E E
C S A L V A T I O N C G N I D
N P S P R I N K L I N G E A N
A T S I R H C S U S E J E D U
S I N C O R R U P T I B L E I
```

# THE ORIGINS OF KING SAUL

Now there was a man of **Benjamin**, whose name was **Kish**, the son of **Abiel**, the son of **Zeror**, the son of **Bechorath**, the son of **Aphiah**, a Benjamite, a mighty **man of power**. And he had a son, whose name was **Saul**, a choice young **man**, and a goodly: and there was not among the children of **Israel** a **goodlier** person than he: from **his shoulders** and upward he was higher than any of the people. And the asses of Kish Saul's father were **lost**. And Kish said to Saul his son, Take now one of the **servants** with thee, and arise, go seek the asses. And he passed through **mount Ephraim**, and passed through the land of **Shalisha**, but they found them not: then they passed through the land of **Shalim**, and there they were not: and he passed through the **land** of the **Benjamites**, but they found them not. And when they were come to the land of **Zuph**, Saul said to his servant that was with him, Come, and let us return; lest my father leave caring for the asses, and take thought for us. And he said unto him, Behold now, there is in this **city** a man of God, and he is an honourable man; all that he saith cometh surely to pass: now let us go thither; **peradventure** he can shew us our way that we should go.

1 SAMUEL 9:1–6

# WORD SEARCH

```
H E A R L B O W H E A G O S T
O S R E I L D O O G Y U R W I
U Z I A H T A R O H C E B E U
D B M K F S K O P H D X E R Q
A U P I Z E T U N L F U N U A
L O R W A E Z N U L H C J T H
E T S O L R K O A M N R A N S
E H H O U A H S T V O I M E I
K Y A K A S N P H R R N I V L
O T T I S O O D E A O E N D A
R O N I H T I Z I T L U S A H
T P H E C P H R A I N I Q R S
T S E T I M A J N E B U M E O
Y I S R A E L O U I M N O P V
A D U N R E W O P F O N A M E
```

# sixteen
## PLACES OF BIBLICAL WARS AND BATTLES

**Canaan** (Joshua 9:1–2)

**Debir** (Joshua 10:38)

**Ebenezer** (1 Samuel 4:1)

**Eglon** (Joshua 10:34)

**Egypt** (2 Kings 24:7)

**Gaza** (Judges 1:18)

**Gibeah** (Judges 20:20)

**Gilboa** (1 Samuel 31:1)

**Hazor** (Joshua 11:10)

**Hebron** (Joshua 10:36)

**Hormah** (Judges 1:17)

**Israel** (2 Samuel 21:15)

**Jericho** (Joshua 6)

**Jerusalem** (2 Kings 24:10)

**Judah** (2 Chronicles 20)

**Lachish** (Joshua 10:31)

**Laish** (Judges 18:27)

**Libnah** (Joshua 10:39)

**Magog** (Revelation 20:8)

**Makkedah** (Joshua 10:10)

**Michmash** (1 Samuel 14:31)

**Moab** (2 Kings 3:5)

**Ziklag** (1 Samuel 30:1)

# WORD SEARCH

```
T P Y G E H D E B H S I A L G
L N C H R O Z A H J E S M A M
G O G A M R S L R Y N R T H A
E L B E N M H Z E M O A B R K
B G O B Y A L A B N J E D U K
J E R I C H O H E R M L J I E
M G J B A G O A D B T R E E D
A L U P N T A L H N I E R R A
O A D E A B Z S R O Z G U E H
B C A Y A J A M O R A D S Z G
L H H E N M G J U E D E A E A
I I Z O H B Y L O B Y B L N Z
G S T C L Z I K L A G I E E I
L H I H E B R O N B O R M B Y
J M E L C A I H A N B I L E T
```

## seventeen 17
# GRACE AND PEACE
# BE MULTIPLIED

**Grace** and **peace** be **multiplied** unto you through the **knowledge** of **God**, and of **Jesus** our **Lord**, according as his **divine power** hath given unto us all things that pertain unto **life** and **godliness**, through the knowledge of him that hath called us to **glory** and **virtue**: whereby are given unto us **exceeding great** and **precious promises**: that by these ye might be **partakers** of the divine **nature**, having **escaped** the **corruption** that is in the **world** through **lust**. And beside this, giving all **diligence**, add to your **faith** virtue; and to virtue knowledge. . . .

2 PETER 1:2–5

# WORD SEARCH

```
W G R E M P R O M I S E S U L
G O F F U G D E P A C S E D D
V I R I G N I D E E C X E I I
E F A L E S C A P O K J I L L
E C E G D E L W O N K E U I I
N T A E R G P C T A N S W G S
I G P R E C I O U S T U O E R
V O P O G O W R F Y D S R N E
I I A O W O Z R D A R U L C K
D T R G R E D U R E I O E E A
V I R T U E R P O R F T L R T
U D E I L P I T L U M A H G R
L E S C A P U I R T G L I K A
S S E N I L D O G A E C A E P
P V I R T U S N U N I C E R P
```

# eighteen

# THREE-SYLLABLE NAMES IN THE BIBLE

Abigail

Abraham

Benjamin

Delilah

Elijah

Gabriel

Gideon

Ichabod

Isaiah

Joanna

Jonathan

Joshua

Lydia

Malachi

Miriam

Naomi

Priscilla

Rebekah

Samuel

Solomon

Timothy

# WORD SEARCH

```
A Z K H A K E B E R M H J P D
D D E L I L A H P Y D V O E B
J O A N N A U K R D Q W N L P
A B N E A D I R I R Y U A I L
C M O N K O O I S O H I T J K
D G E L E B M A C B T T H A M
L L D E M A N I I Z O B A H M
K E I I I H C A L A M I N N A
D U G R E C L M L U I U I O H
J M A B E I W E A T T D Y M A
O A D A A A S D R F B N Y O R
S S Y G E D M X D G G T H L B
H F I M N V R T H J I O P O A
U B M I R I A M W H A I A S I
A A Q R N I M A J N E B D S T
```

# nineteen

# GOD OF. . . (OLD TESTAMENT)

**Abraham** (Genesis 26:24)

<u>**All Flesh**</u> (Jeremiah 32:27)

**Daniel** (Daniel 6:26)

**David** (2 Kings 20:5)

**Elijah** (2 Kings 2:14)

**Forces** (Daniel 11:38)

**Glory** (Psalm 29:3)

**Gods** (Joshua 22:22)

**Heaven** (Genesis 24:3)

**Hezekiah** (2 Chronicles 32:17)

**Hosts** (2 Samuel 5:10)

**Isaac** (Genesis 28:13)

**Israel** (Exodus 5:1)

**Jacob** (Genesis 49:24)

**Jerusalem** (Ezra 7:19)

**Judgment** (Malachi 2:17)

**Knowledge** (1 Samuel 2:3)

<u>**My Life**</u> (Psalm 42:8)

<u>**My Mercy**</u> (Psalm 59:17)

My **Righteousness** (Psalm 4:1)

<u>**My Rock**</u> (2 Samuel 22:3)

**Truth** (Deuteronomy 32:4)

# WORD SEARCH

```
G K L O D P M Y R O C K H S Q
F U I I K M A H A R B A E S T
S M V E I Y G L K D I S A E Y
Z A X D S A L U P K N B V N N
D M I T S F J K E L J M E S O
A O U N L Y T Z R W E Q N U J
N P R E A I E N M L R Y U O A
I A S M T H L G P O U I C E C
E H F G N L Z X D V S A B T O
L G O D S E H B C E A G S H B
H Z R U X A A C M S L R T G C
T Q C J W R J S I O E W S I V
U Y E M V S I X R B M K O R B
R W S E F I L Y M P I L H N N
T B M M Y M E R C Y O R X C K
```

# ABOVE ALL THINGS

But the **end** of all **things** is <u>at hand</u>: be ye therefore **sober**, and **watch** unto **prayer**. And above all things have **fervent charity** among yourselves: for charity shall cover the **multitude** of **sins**. Use **hospitality** one to another without **grudging**. As **every man** hath received the **gift**, even so **minister** the same one to another, as **good stewards** of the **manifold grace** of **God**.

1 PETER 4:7–10

# WORD SEARCH

```
R E T S I N I M A W I P S O H
G M H O S P I T A L I T Y S G
R I C H A R I T O N H A M O M
U N A T H A C F Y A R P D B E
D I F E D H R I S O B G T E N
G A T H A N D G X R E Y A R P
I E N B J F E R V E N T N I M
N G O Y T I R A H C S I N I M
G S I N V E D U T I T L U M A
E D O O G G R U D H F C T A W
Y R E V E O S S Y R I A H C Q
F E R V C E N T H I N N E W D
P R A M A N I F O L D I G O F
E N H Y R T S T E W A R D S I
H O S P G I T G K A W E T Ș G
```

# twenty-one

# ITEMS FOUND IN BIBLICAL DREAMS

**Angel** (Matthew 2:19)

**Barley Bread** (Judges 7:13)

**Baskets** (Genesis 40:16)

**Beasts** (Daniel 7:2–3)

**Birds** (Genesis 40:16–17)

**Blossoms** (Genesis 40:9–10)

**Ears of Corn** (Genesis 41:5)

**East Wind** (Genesis 41:5–6)

**Eleven Stars** (Genesis 37:9)

**Grapes** (Genesis 40:9–10)

**Great Image** (Daniel 2:28–31)

**Great Sea** (Daniel 7:2)

**Horns** (Daniel 7:7)

**Ladder** (Genesis 28:12)

**Moon** (Genesis 37:9)

**Mountain** (Daniel 2:28–35)

**Pharaoh's Cup** (Genesis 40:9–11)

**Rams** (Genesis 31:10)

**Ribs** (Daniel 7:2–5)

**River** (Genesis 41:1)

**Sun** (Genesis 37:9)

**Tent** (Judges 7:13)

**Three Branches** (Genesis 40:9–10)

**Throne** (Daniel 7:7–9)

**Vine** (Genesis 40:9)

**Winds** (Daniel 7:2)

**Wings** (Daniel 7:2–4)

# WORD SEARCH

```
D A E R B Y E L R A B E P S M
R I B A N G E L S N U S H E T
S Q U G R E A T S E A N A P O
R E M B A S K E T S S O R A B
A G R A M S O U N D T R A R L
T A S D N I W F R A I N O G O
S M T R E E S I C B O L H D S
N I W O U N B L S O D O S T S
E T N E T R W A M E R D C K O
V A L M O I I D L N D N U D M
E E E N I V N D S E R G P A S
L R C A K E G E A S T W I N D
E G D Y T R S R W E N O R H T
Z S E H C N A R B E E R H T E
S T S A E B V M O U N T A I N
```

twenty-two

# THE LORD UPHOLDS MY LIFE

**Save me**, O God, by thy **name**, and **judge** me by **thy strength**. Hear my **prayer**, O God; give ear to the **words** of my **mouth**. For **strangers** are risen up **against me**, and **oppressors** seek after my **soul**: they have not set **God** before them. **Selah**. Behold, God is mine **helper**: the **Lord** is with them that **uphold** my soul. He shall **reward evil** unto mine **enemies**: cut them off in thy **truth**. I will freely **sacrifice** unto thee: I will **praise** thy name, O LORD; for it is **good**. For he hath **delivered** me out of all **trouble**: and mine eye hath seen his **desire** upon mine enemies.

PSALM 54:1–7

# WORD SEARCH

```
A U S E L A H B E C S T W P N
C E P A T R O U B L E O J R U
S E V H V B N J I O R M E A P
E G P I O E G G K D L W G Y J
H D R O L L M Y S Y A A F E U
T A A G U F D E J R I M B R D
G M I D O X V B D N R T G J G
N G S F S R O S S E R P P O E
E S E R Y R T T Y R E P L E H
R I H G G N M R N E R I S E D
T O I U Y E T R U F B D S Z B
S T R A N G E R S T G O O D E
Y D E R E V I L E D H T U O M
H D E N E M I E S X F E B G A
T C E S H E C I F I R C A S N
```

## twenty-23-three

# PSALM 115:1–18

Not unto us, **O LORD**, not unto us, but unto thy name give **glory**, for thy **mercy**, and for thy truth's sake. Wherefore should the **heathen** say, Where is now their **God**? But our God is in the **heavens**: he hath done whatsoever he hath pleased. Their **idols** are **silver and gold**, the work of men's hands. They have mouths, but they speak not: eyes have they, but they see not: they have ears, but they hear not: noses have they, but they **smell** not: they have **hands**, but they handle not: **feet** have they, but they walk not: neither speak they through their **throat**. They that make them are like unto them; so is every one that **trusteth** in them. O Israel, trust thou in the LORD: he is their help and their shield. **O house of Aaron**, trust in the LORD: he is their **help** and their **shield**. Ye that fear the LORD, trust in the LORD: he is their help and their shield. The LORD hath been **mindful** of us: he will bless us; he will **bless** the house of Israel; he will bless the house of Aaron. He will bless them that fear the LORD, both **small** and great. The LORD shall **increase** you more and more, you and your children. Ye are **blessed** of the LORD which made heaven and **earth**. The heaven, even the heavens, are the LORD's: but the earth hath he given to the children of men. The dead **praise** not the LORD, neither any that go down into **silence**. But we will bless the LORD from this time forth and for **evermore**. **Praise the LORD**.

# WORD SEARCH

```
D E C N E L I S T A O R H T S
A N C H Y E R O M R E V E B O
D U O L O R D U R D F O L L D
H L P R I W O B I D O L S E R
E T O R A U B L E S S U H S O
P R R G A A S Y G L E F I S L
D U E A D I F R O L D D N E E
L S S O E N S O D E A N E D H
E T A L F H A E E M F I H U T
I E E L W E B R Y S R M T Q E
H T R A H A E Z E V U C A I S
S H C M E V H T O V K O E O I
Q E N S N E V A E H L E H G A
H U I V S N M E R C Y I X O R
C S D N A H E L P R M O S E P
```

# twenty24four

# COUNT ON CHILDREN

Below are scripture passages related to children. Your challenge is to find the *numbers* in the passage. If the scripture is John 3:16–17, you will find 31617 in the grid.

Genesis **3:15–16**

Genesis **18:18–19**

Genesis **25:21–23**

Exodus **13:14–16**

Deuteronomy **11:18–19**

Deuteronomy **32:46–47**

1 Samuel **2:18–19**

Psalm **103:17**

Psalm **107:41**

Psalm **127:3–5**

Psalm **128:2–4**

Psalm **132:12**

Proverbs **31:27–29**

Isaiah **54:13–14**

Matthew **2:16–18**

Matthew **7:11–12**

Matthew **10:21–22**

Matthew **19:13–14**

Mark **7:26–28**

Mark **9:36–37**

Mark **10:14–16**

Luke **9:47–48**

Luke **18:15–17**

Luke **18:29–30**

Acts **2:38–39**

Acts **17:27–28**

Romans **9:10–12**

1 Corinthians **13:11–12**

1 Corinthians **14:20–21**

Colossians **3:20–21**

# WORD SEARCH

```
9  3  8  3  2  3  9  8  1  7  3  6  5  9  4
6  7  3  1  2  7  2  9  2  3  9  1  1  3  2
4  8  9  3  0  1  3  0  0  2  0  8  5  0  9
1  0  2  4  3  5  4  3  2  9  1  2  3  1  8
3  2  4  1  5  1  5  2  4  1  7  6  4  7  6
1  9  8  3  8  8  6  1  1  1  3  9  1  5  2
4  9  7  2  3  1  5  2  7  9  8  2  7  8  1
5  2  6  5  4  8  9  5  0  7  1  2  3  4  2
1  8  7  1  7  2  7  2  8  1  9  3  9  6  3
9  3  0  6  5  4  6  9  1  7  2  7  1  3  1
1  1  1  7  6  1  4  7  0  1  2  3  0  4  0
8  9  8  4  5  5  2  4  3  7  1  6  0  9  8
1  2  2  9  1  0  1  2  1  9  2  3  2  1  3
8  3  4  6  8  6  9  5  7  6  0  9  6  8  2
1  0  8  4  7  4  9  3  4  2  1  1  1  3  1
```

# twenty five

# PHARAOH'S DAUGHTER FINDS MOSES

And there went a man of the **house of Levi**, and took to **wife** a daughter of Levi. And the woman **conceived**, and bare a son: and when she saw him that he was a **goodly child**, she hid him **three** months. And when she could not longer **hide** him, she took for him an **ark** of **bulrushes**, and daubed it with slime and with **pitch**, and put the child therein; and she laid it in the flags by the river's brink. And his sister stood afar off, to wit what would be done to him. And the daughter of **Pharaoh** came down to wash herself at the **river**; and her **maidens** walked along by the river's side; and when she saw the ark among the **flags**, she sent her maid to fetch it. And when she had opened it, she saw the child: and, behold, the **babe** wept. And she had **compassion** on him, and said, This is one of the Hebrews' children. Then said his sister to Pharaoh's **daughter**, Shall I go and call to thee a nurse of the **Hebrew** women, that she may nurse the child for thee? And Pharaoh's daughter said to her, Go. And the maid went and called the child's mother. And Pharaoh's daughter said unto her, Take this child away, and **nurse** it for me, and I will give thee **thy wages**. And the woman took the child, and nursed it. And the child grew, and she brought him unto Pharaoh's daughter, and he became her son. And she called his name **Moses**: and she said, Because I drew him **out of the water**.

EXODUS 2:1–10

# WORD SEARCH

```
W I T G W E R B E H J U I K O
E C P O V T W I C E S M U C H
G O R O O B E T I D F N M P N
E M E D E V I E C N O C Y H U
N P T L W P O X R I V E R A R
Y A H Y A F L O G H E X I R S
T S G C S S E S O M T I F A E
H S U H I V E L F O E S U O H
O I A I Z E G H Y F E D I H S
U O D L N O X A W O L D Z O U
H N U D S E F I W Y E A E L R
G E E L K F O U N J A U G A L
A D X B R U M A I D E N S S U
C R E T A W E H T F O T U O B
S T A D Y B K S E G A W Y H T
```

# A CHANGED LIFE

No life journey is a straight path. Some people from the Bible made changes that changed the direction of their journey for good. In this puzzle, each hidden word will bend at an angle instead of appearing in one straight line.

**Andrew** (John 1:40)

**Apollos** (Acts 18:24–25)

**Bartimaeus** (Mark 10:46–52)

**Cornelius** (Acts 10)

**Crispus** (Acts 18:8)

**Darius** (Daniel 6:25–27)

**David** (1 Samuel 16:13)

Ethiopian **eunuch** (Acts 8:27–37)

**Lydia** (Acts 16:14–15)

**Mary** Magdalene (Mark 16:9

**Matthew** (Matthew 9:9)

**Naaman** (2 Kings 5:11–15)

**Nebuchadnezzar**
(Daniel 3:28–29)

**Nicodemus** (John 3:1–21)

**Philip** (John 1:43)

Philippian **jailor** (Acts 16:23–34)

**Publican** (Luke 18:13–14)

**Rahab** (Joshua 2:1–9)

**Ruth** (Ruth 1:16)

**Samaritan woman**
(John 4:7, 29)

**Saul of Tarsus** (Acts 9:4–6)

**Sergius** Paulus (Acts 13:7–12)

**Simon Peter** (John 1:42)

**Thief on Cross** (Luke 23:39–42)

**Zacchaeus** (Luke 19:8)

# WORD SEARCH

```
C O M I S A N D R S A M A R I
U H N C R O S S H E M L Y D T
B S A P N F K D A R W A B I A
E U L D E O S B A H I C T A N
N E B I N T F U C A Z U K T W
C A U Q C E E E E R Y Z S H O
O M P W Y A Z R I A W A J E M
R I T R A B N Z E H H C S W A
N N L L O P A C A U T C F U N
E A Z O H T U R F R N D Q R I
L M S X S V R I W U I Y O H G
P I A U S U P S C V R L F E R
I S U A M K J H L M A A I I E
L B A S N E D O C I N D M A S
I H P U L O F T A R S U S A J
```

# LINEAGE OF JESUS

The book of the generation of <u>**Jesus Christ**</u>, the son of **David**, the son of **Abraham.** Abraham begat **Isaac**; and Isaac begat **Jacob**; and Jacob begat **Judas** and his brethren; and Judas begat **Phares** and Zara of Thamar; and Phares begat **Esrom**; and Esrom begat Aram; and Aram begat **Aminadab**; and Aminadab begat **Naasson**; and Naasson begat Salmon; and Salmon **begat** Booz of **Rachab**; and Booz begat <u>**Obed of Ruth**</u>; and Obed begat **Jesse**; and Jesse begat David the king; and David the king begat **Solomon** of her that had been the wife of Urias; and Solomon begat Roboam; and Roboam begat Abia; and **Abia** begat Asa; and Asa begat Josaphat; and Josaphat begat **Joram**; and Joram begat Ozias; and **Ozias** begat Joatham; and **Joatham** begat Achaz; and **Achaz** begat Ezekias; and **Ezekias** begat Manasses; and **Manasses** begat Amon; and Amon begat **Josias**; and Josias begat **Jechonias** and his brethren, about the time they were carried away to Babylon: and after they were brought to Babylon, Jechonias begat Salathiel; and Salathiel begat **Zorobabel**; and Zorobabel begat Abiud; and Abiud begat **Eliakim**; and Eliakim begat **Azor**; and Azor begat Sadoc; and **Sadoc** begat Achim; and Achim begat Eliud; and Eliud begat Eleazar; and Eleazar begat **Matthan**; and Matthan begat Jacob; and Jacob begat **Joseph** the husband of **Mary**, of whom was born Jesus, who is called Christ.

MATTHEW 1:1–16

# WORD SEARCH

```
M J O A T H A M M A T T H A N
I E B Z O L E B A B O R O Z M
K C O M A R O J B A H C A R A
A H C E I O B E D O F R U T H
I O A Z L E S S I R O C H S A
L N J Y G R X S V S S H P I R
E I A A O N O E A M A F K R B
S A T M A S H Z D V I A A H A
E S B J I Q U I A N Z E C C A
S Z A I O N A A S S O N O S I
S X E I A S A Y R A M S B U Z
A Z I K S U E D J J U D A S P
N U N G I O H P A P H A R E S
A C H A Z A J Z H B S U O J P
M S A D O C S N O M O L O S M
```

# PAUL IN CORINTH (ACTS 18)

| | |
|---|---|
| Aquila | Justus |
| Baptized | Paul |
| Believed | Priscilla |
| <u>Chief Ruler</u> | Sabbath |
| Corinth | Spirit |
| Crispus | Synagogue |
| Gentiles | Teaching |
| Greeks | Tentmakers |
| <u>Jesus Christ</u> | Testified |
| Jews | Worshipped |

# WORD SEARCH

```
P A U D W O R S H I P P E D P
D C O E A Q U I L J S C U A J
E P R I S A T E N U Y S G U E
Z S A F L J E W P S G Y O G S
I T T I R I P S J T R N G N U
T E U T E S I F U U E A A I S
P Q C S B R L C S S E G N H C
A B H E C I R U T J Y O Y C H
B S I T E N T M A K E R S A R
A A L L I C S I R P S W C E I
I B C H I E R O W K S R S T S
T B D E V E I L E B I I P S T
P A U N C H I E F R U L E R Q
A T A E M A R K H T N I R O C
B H P T X G E N T I L E S E J
```

# DANIEL IS PROMOTED

Then the king **Nebuchadnezzar** fell upon his **face**, and **worshipped** Daniel, and commanded that they should offer an **oblation** and <u>sweet odours</u> unto him. The **king** answered unto **Daniel**, and said, Of a **truth** it is, that your God is a <u>**God of gods**</u>, and a <u>**Lord of kings**</u>, and a **revealer** of **secrets**, seeing thou couldest reveal this secret. Then the king made Daniel a <u>**great man**</u>, and gave him many great **gifts**, and made him **ruler** over the whole province of **Babylon**, and **chief** of the **governors** over all the <u>**wise men**</u> of Babylon. Then Daniel requested of the king, and he set **Shadrach**, **Meshach**, and **Abednego**, over the affairs of the province of Babylon: but Daniel sat in the gate of the king.

DANIEL 2:46–49

# WORD SEARCH

```
R E L A E V E R W B S T L C X
D N O I T A L B O K W R O E R
B G O V E R N O R S E U R F A
B A B Y L O N A S U E T D M Z
C S H C A R D A H S T H O E Z
A S J H N S I J I R O D F S E
M T L I V H L K P T D N K H N
N E I E K O P U P R O A I A D
G R N F I I O P E E U M N C A
I C F G N N H J D L R T G H H
F E S R G F A N M U S A S T C
T S X E V F U D E R N E G Y U
S W C Q N E M E S I W R R T B
F A I B P A B E D N E G O Y E
F J R N F S D O G F O D O G N
```

# COURAGEOUS MIDWIVES

And the **king of Egypt** spake to the **Hebrew** midwives, of which the name of the one was **Shiphrah**, and the name of the other **Puah**: and he said, When ye do the **office** of a **midwife** to the Hebrew **women**, and see them upon the **stools**; if it <u>**be a son**</u>, then ye shall **kill** him: but if it be a **daughter**, then <u>**she shall live**</u>. But the midwives **feared** God, and did not as the king of Egypt **commanded** them, but saved the men children alive. And the king of Egypt called for the midwives, and said unto them, Why have ye <u>**done this thing**</u>, and have saved the men **children** alive? And the midwives said unto **Pharaoh**, Because the Hebrew women are not as the Egyptian women; for they are **lively**, and are **delivered** ere the midwives come in unto them. Therefore God <u>**dealt well**</u> with the midwives: and the **people** multiplied, and **waxed** very **mighty**. And it <u>**came to pass**</u>, because the midwives feared God, that he made them **houses**.

EXODUS 1:15–21

*Secret message:*

\_\_\_\_\_  \_\_\_\_\_  \_\_  _____  \_\_\_\_\_  \_\_\_\_\_

\_\_\_\_\_  _____  \_\_\_\_\_  \_\_\_\_  \_\_\_\_\_

\_\_\_\_\_  \_\_\_\_\_  \_\_\_\_\_?

# WORD SEARCH

```
W H A F S E S U O H E B R E W
T C D N E H D E L I V E R E D
S P O E T A I L A L N D I D M
H R F M X P R P L S I P H A I
E E F O M A Y E H R L V A O G
S T I W H A W G D R H O E A H
H H C T C T N H E A A F O L T
A G E T L E R D T F H H E T Y
L U M A I C A M E T O P A S S
L A E B D W I V E D S G C H L
L D O N E T H I S T H I N G L
I O S P H A R A O H E N O I I
V T T O U K S E F I W D I M K
E I L P L P E O P L E T H E B
A C H I L D R E N B Y B O Y S
```

## PSALM 4:1–8

<u>Hear me</u> when I call, O God of my **righteousness**: thou hast **enlarged** me when I was in **distress**; have **mercy** upon me, and <u>hear my prayer</u>. O ye <u>sons of men</u>, how long will ye turn my **glory** into **shame**? how long will ye love **vanity**, and seek after leasing? **Selah**. But know that the LORD hath set **apart** him that is **godly** for himself: the LORD will hear when I **call** unto him. Stand in awe, and sin not: **commune** with your own **heart** upon your **bed**, and be still. Selah. Offer the **sacrifices** of righteousness, and put your **trust** in the LORD. There be many that say, Who will **shew** us any good? LORD, lift thou up the light of thy **countenance** upon us. Thou hast put **gladness** in my heart, more than in the time that their corn and their wine increased. I will both lay me down <u>in peace</u>, and sleep: for thou, LORD, only makest me dwell in **safety**.

# WORD SEARCH

```
E S S E N S U O E T H G I R E R
R H S E O U R E C H T R A E H
G A H N T R A P A D I D E S W
D L E L V A H M E R C Y R A E
O E O A B T E Y P I O N E C H
L S B R U J A N N T U E Y R S
P H Y G Y L R E I S N K A I L
O P L E N B M J S C T S R F N
F O D D I F E E S O E S P I U
V C O H O X R A H M N E Y C Y
E A G S Y T F R A M A N M E R
T H N B S E S T M U N D R S S
U O L I T E G U E N C A A H S
S E D Y T A H W R E E L E U E
Z L L A C Y S U O T I G H L S
```

# BIBLE MEN WITH MULTIPLE MATES

**Abijah** (2 Chronicles 13:21)

**Abram** (Genesis 16:3)

**Ahab** (2 Kings 10:1)

**Ashur** (1 Chronicles 4:5)

**Belshazzar** (Daniel 5:1–3)

**David** (2 Samuel 3:2–5)

**Elkanah** (1 Samuel 1:1–2)

**Esau** (Genesis 36:2)

**Gideon** (Judges 8:30)

**Jacob** (Genesis 35:22–26)

**Jehoiachin** (2 Kings 24:15)

**Jehoram** (2 Chronicles 21:9–14)

**Jerahmeel** (1 Chronicles 2:25–26)

**Joash** (2 Chronicles 24:2–3)

**Lamech** (Genesis 4:19)

**Machir** (1 Chronicles 7:15)

**Rehoboam** (2 Chronicles 11:18–21)

**Shaharaim** (1 Chronicles 8:8–9)

**Solomon** (1 Kings 11:1–3)

**Zedekiah** (Jeremiah 38:17–23)

# WORD SEARCH

```
C R E A M O N J E H O R A M L
B A O L S Z A I S T A Z D S E
A Z J M O H N T A B I J A H M
N Z S H I C U H U E R T V A A
J A J O A S H R I N T O I H O
E H C H A N A K L E L A D A B
H S Z M R E H O A G B O E R O
O L E C N A B R M O I N T A H
I E D S O H U N E J U D O I E
A B E L M R I H C A M I E M R
C H K C O N T B H J A P S O L
H E I B L S A U O N R H A I N
I N A S O T R E T C B R A V E
N O H W S H A M P O A L E B Z
P H A L E E M H A R E J T G I
```

# thirty-33-three

## PETER'S SERMON

And it shall come to pass in the <u>**last days**</u>, saith **God**, I will **pour** out of my **Spirit** upon all **flesh**: and your **sons** and your **daughters** shall **prophesy**, and your **young men** shall **see visions**, and your **old** men shall **dream** dreams: and on my **servants** and on my **handmaidens** I will pour out in those **days** of my Spirit; and they shall prophesy: and I will shew **wonders** in **heaven above**, and **signs** in the **earth beneath**; blood, and **fire**, and **vapour** of **smoke**: the **sun** shall be turned into **darkness**, and the **moon** into **blood**, before that **great** and **notable** day of the Lord come: and it shall come to **pass**, that whosoever shall **call** on the **name** of the **Lord** shall be **saved**.

Acts 2:17–21

# WORD SEARCH

```
P D A R K N E S S O W O G F L
O H D R O L W E K O M S L N A
U E P D V A P O U R Y E D O G
R S A Y P R O P H E S Y N T R
G Y U O N E V A E H F O E A E
S H A N D M A I D E N S M B A
F I R E T I R I P S E E A L T
S S R E D N O W Y L B O N E S
S N G I S S M A E R D E V A S
H A O Y N M D A U G H T E R S
A L D I O T A T O N O O L B A
D B A S S U U H T A E N E B P
H T R A E I N G U A D O O L B
C O L L A C V G P A V V E O B
S E R V A N T S S I E U O P M
```

# TWO-SYLLABLE NAMES
# IN THE BIBLE

Aaron

Adam

Anna

Caleb

David

Esther

Ezra

Isaac

Jacob

Jesse

Joseph

Leah

Micah

Mary

Moses

Nathan

Noah

Omar

Peter

Rachel

Sarah

Stephen

Simon

Thomas

Titus

# WORD SEARCH

```
A D G C A Y H P E S O J P O N
G A E M O S E S V G M Y R A M
T D R Y N E H P E T S U T I T
H X G O H K I I L P D H B J S
O C G M N A E E H C A A S I E
M S F A O M A A N N A X E B T
A S A R M H R R T E H L O H T
S D V F I A G Z Y A J G E N R
W Z F F S Q U E C D B D W B E
H O J E S S E I H J D L M N H
F R G A D A M V D S A I N C T
H E L K C C Z V N D E N V H S
H T L E F O N L E H C A R A E
U E J K P D B Z E F H K L O D
I P F E G V Q C D H D Y R N C
```

# NOAH LEAVES THE ARK

And God remembered **Noah**, and every living thing, and **all the cattle** that was with him in the ark: and God made a wind to pass over the **earth**, and the waters **assuaged**; the **fountains** also of the deep and the windows of **heaven** were stopped, and the **rain** from heaven was restrained; and the waters returned from off the earth continually: and after the end of the **hundred and fifty** days the waters were **abated**. And the ark rested in the **seventh month**, on the **seventeenth** day of the month, upon the mountains of **Ararat**. And the waters decreased continually until the tenth month: in the tenth month, on the first day of the month, were the tops of the **mountains** seen. And it came to pass at the end of forty days, that Noah opened the window of the ark which he had made: and he sent forth a **raven**, which went forth **to and fro**, until the waters were dried up from off the earth. Also he sent forth a **dove** from him, to see if the waters were abated from off the face of the **ground**; but the dove found no rest for the **sole** of her foot, and she returned unto him into the ark, for the waters were on the **face** of the whole earth: then he put forth his **hand**, and took her, and pulled her in unto him into the ark. And he stayed yet other **seven** days; and again he sent forth the dove out **of the ark**; and the dove came in to him in the evening; and, lo, in her mouth was an **olive leaf** pluckt off: so Noah knew that the waters were abated from off the earth.

GENESIS 8:1–11

# WORD SEARCH

```
B Y R E A Y H N K O P M E D R
H T N E E T N E V E S O B I E
O F A E L E V I L O H U L K N
H I A L S W U J N E E N D H E
A F D C L N D E B L A T N T V
O D E X E T I C R O V A U N E
N N T A F N H A E S E I O O S
H A A R E O I E T A N N R M S
E D B V I N U D C N R S G H O
G E A R A R A T H A U T E T U
D R C O R F D N A O T O H N N
N D M O U N A I D G S T F E B
A N E V O D Q U T I A D L V E
H U J S K R A E H T F O N E A
S H Y D U D E G A U S S A S D
```

# FIVE CROSSES #1

In this puzzle, you will find five-letter words that are commonly found in the Bible. Your search will be aided by the fact that each word has a partner word that crosses its center, forming either an "x" or a "+" shape.

| | |
|---|---|
| Altar | Loves |
| Angel | Pride |
| Arise | Reign |
| Bride | Serve |
| Covet | Shall |
| Curse | Shame |
| Demon | Slave |
| Dream | Speak |
| Faith | Storm |
| Feast | Teach |
| Fruit | Truth |
| Giant | Water |
| Glory | Weary |
| Image | Woman |
| Light | Write |

# WORD SEARCH

```
E N S M K N T R M B V A E O I
R O A T O A E A X W S H J K T
I K U M D H E S T E G E T E S
P F E Y O R L P R R F I V D C
S D T U D W B V S U U O M O V
H T I A F A E K N R C T C B L
D O R W S H P T F E P F H N E
U W W P E C N A L T A R E S P
Q E F L L A H S I A U Y I L K
C Z B M I E R O T W R R E D A
A K S G T T T Y S O A N D H E
W N P H M S I U L P R E I G N
S F G U A F E G A M I M R S A
R I H E X M Y O V B E T B D G
L J F N L C E Z E A W R S I H
```

# JOSHUA RENEWS THE COVENANT

Then **Joshua** built an **altar** unto the Lord God of Israel in **mount Ebal**, as Moses the servant of the Lord commanded the **children** of **Israel**, as it is written in the book of the law of Moses, an altar of **whole stones**, over which no man hath lift up any **iron**: and they offered thereon burnt **offerings** unto the Lord, and sacrificed **peace** offerings. And he wrote there upon the stones a copy of **the law** of Moses, which he wrote in the presence of the children of Israel. And all Israel, and their **elders**, and **officers**, and their **judges**, stood on this side the **ark** and on that side before the **priests** the **Levites**, which bare the ark of the covenant of the Lord, as well the stranger, as he that was born among them; half of them over against mount **Gerizim**, and half of them over against mount Ebal; as **Moses** the servant of the Lord had commanded before, that they should bless the people of Israel. And afterward he **read** all the words of the law, the **blessings** and **cursings**, according to all that is **written** in the book of the law.

JOSHUA 8:30–34

# WORD SEARCH

```
A O F F I C E R S D R A T L A
K Y B T G D X D B F E C A E P
H G L H S E N O T S E L O H W
I G E E E C X F M D J D G N C
K H S L F Q P F O E U G D B H
H F S A M G R E S V D N O R I
J D I W I V I R E S G V B D L
O F N O Z F E I S A E D A D D
S L G P I N S N E F S E S C R
H E S I R E T G P S R E D L E
U A Y U E T S S T R E F G B N
A R R K G T U L E V I T E S C
A S D K F I S G N I S R U C B
D I E T Y R J K M N B V C Z D
B X D G U W L A B E T N U O M
```

# thirty-eight 38
# THINGS FOUND IN
# THE LAND OF ISRAEL

| | |
|---|---|
| Barley | Honey |
| Brass | Houses |
| Bread | Iron |
| <u>Brooks of Water</u> | <u>Oil Olive</u> |
| <u>Fig Trees</u> | Pomegranates |
| Flocks | Silver |
| Fountains | Stones |
| Gold | Valleys |
| Herds | Vines |
| Hills | Wheat |

# WORD SEARCH

```
R E V L I S C R A H E R D S T
I R O V E L S Y E L L A V R S
S E T A N A R G E M O P E N W
T B O S L L I H R L W T H F L
O R E A I D Y R E B A R L E Y
N P O M T F G A O W M A T S E
E T H I E L D U F N G O L N D
S B O R V O S O I S T D W I P
W C N E I C S R G D A S V A E
H A E G L K C L T E O S R T I
E R Y I O S H U R N V A V N E
A L A O L L P B E W I R T U T
T E R L I Y D F E L N B C O K
C B A H O U S E S A E M E F O
H S T L I H O O L H S A L Y N
```

*thirty* **39** *nine*

# THE HOPE IN YOU

For the **eyes** of the **Lord** are over the **righteous**, and his **ears** are **open** unto their **prayers**: but the **face** of the Lord is against them that do **evil**. And who is he that will **harm** you, if ye be **followers** of that which is good? But and if ye **suffer** for righteousness' sake, **happy** are ye: and be not **afraid** of their **terror**, neither be **troubled**; but **sanctify** the Lord **God** in your **hearts**: and be **ready** always to give an **answer** to every man that **asketh** you a **reason** of the **hope** that is in you with **meekness** and **fear**.

1 PETER 3:12–15

# WORD SEARCH

```
L O R F E V D E L B U O R T R
A H E E N K E E M D O H O G E
F E A A R F O L L O W E R S A
T R E R T R O U E G E V R F S
S E Y E M L O R V H O P E A A
R I G A N E A R I O P S T C S
H S U F F E R S L S T R A E H
A A R R A S P E U H E E R E T
R N E A R P Y O A H H Y U S E
H C A I A E E F A E C A F X K
A T S D S T H A R O P R P O S
P I O A H A N S W E R P Y P A
P F N G R E L O R D U O R T Y
E Y I F O L L O I E T H G I R
F R E A D Y A S S E N K E E M
```

# PRAYER CHANGES THINGS

Prayer has a history of changing circumstances. Find the names of people who prayed in faith. In this puzzle, each hidden word will bend at an angle instead of appearing in one straight line.

**Abraham** (Genesis 15:2)

**Daniel** (Daniel 2:17–18)

**David** (2 Samuel 23:10–13)

**Disciples** (Acts 1:13–14)

**Elijah** (1 Kings 17:20–22)

**Elisha** (2 Kings 6:17–18)

**Ezra** (Ezra 9:6)

**Gideon** (Judges 6:36)

**Habakkuk** (Habakkuk 1:2–4)

**Hannah** (1 Samuel 10:11)

**Hezekiah** (2 Kings 19:15–19)

**Isaac** (Genesis 25:21)

**Jabez** (1 Chronicles 4:10)

**Jacob** (Genesis 32:11)

**Jeremiah** (Jeremiah 42:2)

**Jesus** (Matthew 6:9)

**Job** (Job 42:1–6)

**Joel** (Joel 1:1)

**Joshua** (Joshua 7:6–9)

**Manasseh** (2 Chronicles 33:12–13)

**Moses** (Exodus 15:24–25)

**Nehemiah** (Nehemiah 1:4–11)

**Paul** (Acts 28:8)

**Peter** (Acts 9:40)

**Samson** (Judges 15:18)

**Stephen** (Acts 7:59)

**Zacharias** (Luke 1:13)

# WORD SEARCH

```
I S H A P D J O T D S H P A U
L A Y Z E B A B I R A A V M L
E W B M A N A V Q T I N N A H
J U K R U A U J E E R S D F G
C S I D A S G P A R A B A E N
I L M H I S H I S T E H Y M O
P D A W H E K A D F P H C P S
L M N A E H R J E V H M A A H
E B I J L Z C G O C E L T I Z
S M H A B A J A N X N J O S M
E H E N F S K U C E H W L H E
L E I Z E I U K V O C E X U R
J P N J A E S S U L B A Z A E
O C A M L O J E H K I S A E J
E L D I J A H C S O M H A I K
```

# MOSES RETURNS TO EGYPT

And **Moses** went and **returned** to Jethro his **father in law**, and said unto him, **Let me go**, I **pray** thee, and return unto my **brethren** which are in **Egypt**, and see whether they be yet **alive**. And **Jethro** said to Moses, Go in **peace**. And the LORD said unto Moses in **Midian**, Go, return into Egypt: for all the **men** are **dead** which sought thy **life**. And Moses took his **wife** and his **sons**, and set them upon an ass, and he returned to the **land** of Egypt: and Moses took the **rod** of God in his **hand**. And the LORD said unto Moses, When thou goest to return into Egypt, see that thou do all those **wonders** before **Pharaoh**, which I have put in thine hand: but I will **harden** his **heart**, that he shall not let the people go.

EXODUS 4:18–21

# WORD SEARCH

```
D Y A R P E S P H A R A O H R
L C F J F D G N A I D I M Z E
E F B E G J K E N B E V D N T
T D S T G R T M D F A W R E U
M V R H W Y H V G F D U Q R R
E D E R A A L I V E E F T H N
G I D O O I L P D F N F B T E
O K N Y U D N N G D N A L E D
A D O F C B T R I S E T Q R H
S S W H A R D E N R T E N B J
R N T T Y S T P Y G E J F Y K
Y T O U E U I E U Y M H U I Y
N J K S J I O A I U E A T T W
J K O G F V N C T R A E H A B
A M S Y E T Y E F I L S D F F
```

# POOL OF SILOAM (JOHN 9)

Anointed

Blind Man

Clay

Disciples

Eyes

Jesus

Jews

Light of the World

Miracles

Neighbours

Parents

Pharisees

Pool of Siloam

Sabbath

Seeing

Sinned

Spittle

Wash

Works of God

# WORD SEARCH

```
B  L  S  J  E  S  E  S  E  L  C  A  R  I  M
L  I  S  I  W  O  R  K  S  O  F  G  O  D  H
I  G  I  G  N  I  E  E  S  E  Y  Y  A  W  S
N  H  N  B  L  N  S  W  I  L  A  I  P  S  R
H  T  H  S  E  Y  E  J  E  L  H  G  I  L  U
K  O  T  S  E  J  E  D  C  Y  F  R  O  W  O
S  F  A  N  E  I  G  N  A  M  D  N  I  L  B
A  T  B  W  H  A  S  D  S  A  B  B  A  S  H
W  H  B  S  W  U  J  E  L  T  T  I  P  S  G
H  E  A  J  S  Q  A  N  O  I  N  T  E  D  I
N  W  S  E  D  I  S  C  I  P  L  E  S  W  E
I  O  J  E  W  J  R  T  T  I  P  S  R  A  N
E  R  A  S  E  E  S  I  R  A  H  P  S  A  W
E  L  H  M  A  O  L  I  S  F  O  L  O  O  P
S  D  P  A  N  O  I  N  T  F  E  N  N  I  S
```

# GROWING UP

For when for the time ye **ought** to be **teachers**, ye have need that one teach you again which be the first **principles** of the **oracles** of God; and are become such as have need of **milk**, and not of <u>**strong meat**</u>. For every one that useth milk is unskilful in the **word** of **righteousness**: for he is a **babe**. But strong meat **belongeth** to them that are of <u>**full age**</u>, even those who by **reason** of use have their **senses** exercised to **discern** both good and **evil**. Therefore leaving the principles of the **doctrine** of **Christ**, let us go on unto **perfection**; not **laying** again the **foundation** of **repentance** from <u>**dead works**</u>, and of **faith** toward God.

HEBREWS 5:12–6:1

# WORD SEARCH

```
N S E N S E S L A T I G R I M
O T S D R N O I T A D N U O F
I U G E H T D C R E N I T A S
T E C A N C K B Z M O Y S G E
C E L D O S A N I G P A I M L
E C A W L B U L E N S L R I C
F N M O E G K O D O U G H T A
R A E R N O S A E R L Y C E R
E T G K Q U I T H T I A F A O
P N A S B R A N L S H W E C T
S E L P I C N I R P L G M H Y
A P L A G R V E W R A N I E G
G E U H T E G N O L E B C R K
I R F E L A K Y R Q U I N S C
L E N I R T C O D I S C E R N
```

# GOD OF. . . (NEW TESTAMENT)

**Abraham** (Matthew 22:32)

<u>**All Comfort**</u> (2 Corinthians 1:3)

<u>**All Grace**</u> (1 Peter 5:10)

**Glory** (Acts 7:2)

**Heaven** (Revelation 11:13)

**Hope** (Romans 15:13)

**Isaac** (Matthew 22:32)

**Israel** (Matthew 15:31)

**Jacob** (Matthew 22:32)

**Love** (2 Corinthians 13:11)

<u>**Our Fathers**</u> (Acts 3:13)

<u>**Our Lord Jesus**</u> Christ (Ephesians 1:17)

**Patience** (Romans 15:5)

**Peace** (Romans 15:33)

<u>**The Earth**</u> (Revelation 11:4)

The <u>**Holy Prophets**</u> (Revelation 22:6)

<u>**The Jews**</u> (Romans 3:29)

<u>**The Living**</u> (Mark 12:27)

<u>**This People**</u> of Israel (Acts 13:17)

<u>**Thy Fathers**</u> (Acts 7:32)

# WORD SEARCH

```
W X M N H T R A E E H T O N A
G L B I K J F D S A V Q U B L
N K Y S H E A V E N X O R P J
I J T R O F M O C L L A L A E
V H S A L L Y N M L H P O U C
I G C E Y D A E C A E P R L N
L R A L P C U R M N N Y D M E
E E A U R N Y I H O L L J U I
H D S R O M R E S W E J E H T
T H I S P E O P L E I A S O A
W E R T H U L I O P H C U R P
Q H O P E M G N B V G O S X Z
S R E H T A F Y H T F B A S D
K J H G S R E H T A F R U O L
A L L G R A C E T Y U O I E A
```

# A PRAYER FOR ISRAEL

**Brethren**, my heart's desire and **prayer** to God for **Israel** is, that they might be saved. For I bear them record that they have a <u>**zeal of God**</u>, but not according to **knowledge**. For they being **ignorant** of God's **righteousness**, and going about to **establish** their own righteousness, have not **submitted** themselves unto the righteousness of God. For **Christ** is the end of the law for righteousness to every one that **believeth**. For Moses describeth the righteousness which is <u>**of the law**</u>, that the man which doeth those things shall live by them. But the righteousness which is of **faith** speaketh on this **wise**, Say not in thine heart, Who shall ascend into **heaven**? (that is, to bring Christ down from above:) or, Who shall descend <u>**into the deep**</u>? (that is, to bring up Christ again from the dead.) But what saith it? The word is nigh thee, even in thy mouth, and in thy heart: that is, the <u>**word of faith**</u>, which we **preach**; that if thou shalt **confess** with thy mouth the Lord Jesus, and shalt believe <u>**in thine heart**</u> that God hath raised him from the dead, thou shalt be **saved**. For with the heart man believeth unto righteousness; and with the mouth confession is made unto **salvation**. For the scripture saith, Whosoever believeth on him shall not be **ashamed**.

ROMANS 10:1–11

# WORD SEARCH

```
A B R E G T N A R O N G I N P
R U K X A E D E T T I M B U S
D T N U S L E S T A B L I S H
E R O I N E V A E H U O D A T
M A W H T I A F F O D R O W E
A E L B C W S O A N T J G N V
H H E L O A P R V I E U F O E
S E D E N L S R A U T G O I I
A N G A F E Z A E E Q H L T L
H I E D E H D I V Y L E A A E
C H R I S T E C K E A T E V B
A T F A S F H G O U D R Z L G
E N I N T O T H E D E E P A R
R I B R E T H R E N G A M S E
P S S E N S U O E T H G I R T
```

# KING ME

And it came to pass, when **Samuel** was old, that he made his **sons** judges over Israel. Now the name of his **firstborn** was **Joel**; and the name of his second, **Abiah**: they were judges in **Beer-sheba**. And his sons **walked not** in his ways, but **turned aside** after **lucre**, and **took bribes**, and **perverted judgment**. Then all the **elders of Israel** gathered themselves together, and came to Samuel unto **Ramah**, and said unto him, Behold, thou art old, and thy sons walk not in **thy ways**: now make us a **king to judge** us like all the **nations**. But the thing displeased Samuel, when they said, Give us a king to judge us. And Samuel **prayed** unto the Lord. And the Lord said unto Samuel, **Hearken** unto the voice of the people in all that they say unto thee: for they have not rejected thee, but they have **rejected me**, that I should not **reign** over them.

1 Samuel 8:1–7

# WORD SEARCH

```
D I Z X J A J Y D A N I A N L
E H T O O K B R I B E S O R E
T T H X E I G I E N O M K O A
R N Y O L N B C A N W S H B R
E E W P S G N Q S H E E U T S
V M A S W T E R F D R M N S I
R G Y N O O K T I B L D T R F
E D S O O J R S A M U E L I O
P U H I S U A K Z X L T R F S
Y J A T H D E N X E R C U L R
L D M A E G H V G V I E G P E
L E A N R E K L B I K J X R D
O F R Y A B E H S R E E B U L
H U P L U N K D E Y A R P B E
T O N D E K L A W B I R D S Q
```

# BY HIM

For **by him** were all things **created**, that are in **heaven**, and that are in **earth**, **visible** and **invisible**, whether they be **thrones**, or **dominions**, or **principalities**, or **powers**: **all things** were created by him, and **for him**: and he is **before** all things, and by him all things **consist**. And he is the **head** of the **body**, the **church**: who is the beginning, the **firstborn** from the **dead**; that in all things he might have the **preeminence**.

Colossians 1:16–18

# WORD SEARCH

```
B Y H E C N E N I M E E R P H
C H U R C H U Y T A E R C E A
P O V I S I B L E H E A A D F
F N R O B T S R I F A V V N I
S C H U R Y B O D W E R H T A
N S E N O R H T I N M O D H L
O F O F O R H I M I M O D R L
I D V P D E A D M N A E H O T
N L A A O D E T A E R C E N H
I T H E H W E L B I S I V N I
M R I T H A E T S I S N O C N
O P R Y D O B R I N I M O D G
D A B E F O R E S M E E R P S
E P R I N C I P A L I T I E S
I N V I S I D O M I R O F E B
```

# SHHH. . . WE'RE BUILDING THE TEMPLE

And it **came to pass** in the four **hundred** and **eightieth** year after the children of Israel were come out of the <u>**land of Egypt**</u>, in the fourth year of Solomon's **reign** over **Israel**, in the <u>**month Zif**</u>, which is the **second** month, that he **began** to **build** the <u>**house of the Lord**</u>. And the house which **king Solomon** built for the Lord, the **length** thereof was **threescore** cubits, and the breadth thereof twenty **cubits**, and the **height** thereof thirty cubits. . . . And the house, when it was in building, was **built** of **stone** made **ready** before it was **brought** thither: so that there was neither <u>**hammer nor axe**</u> nor any <u>**tool of iron**</u> **heard** in the house, **while** it was in building.

1 Kings 6:1–2, 7

*Secret message:*

\_\_\_\_\_ \_\_\_\_\_ \_\_\_\_\_ \_\_\_\_\_ \_\_\_\_\_ \_\_\_\_\_

\_\_\_\_\_ \_\_\_\_\_ \_\_\_\_\_ \_\_\_\_\_ \_\_\_\_\_

\_\_\_\_\_ \_\_\_\_\_ \_\_\_\_\_ \_\_\_\_\_?

# WORD SEARCH

```
K H O S W M A M O N T H Z I F
E I G H T I E T H L E A R S I
N Y N Y B I E A R S L M D I D
H L K G U T B I N S I M G S O
E L A O I O M U S T H E O N S
I P E N L O N A C O W R D C O
G N S T D L P R U N L N C T I
H O U S E O F T H E L O R D N
T E G T T F F H Y E T R M N H
E M A E P I L E E D O A F O U
T H M R B R E I G N A X E C N
L A O E D O R D I Y N E J E D
C E G L E N G T H R P U R S R
S A E R O C S E E R H T A L E
N B R O U G H T L I U B E M D
```

# JONAH DEFIES GOD

Now the **word of the LORD** came unto **Jonah** the **son of Amittai,** saying, Arise, go to **Nineveh**, that great city, and cry against it; for their **wickedness** is come up before me. But Jonah rose up to flee unto **Tarshish** from the presence of the LORD, and went down to **Joppa**; and he found a **ship** going to Tarshish: so he paid the **fare** thereof, and went down into it, to go with them unto Tarshish from the presence of the LORD. But the LORD sent out **a great wind** into the sea, and there was a mighty **tempest** in the sea, so that the ship was like to be **broken.** Then the **mariners** were afraid, and cried every man unto his god, and cast forth the **wares** that were in the ship into the sea, to lighten it of them. But Jonah was gone down into the sides of the ship; and he lay, and was fast **asleep**. So the **shipmaster** came to him, and said unto him, What meanest thou, O sleeper? arise, call upon thy God, if so be that God will think upon us, that we **perish** not. And they said every one to his fellow, Come, and let us **cast lots**, that we may know for whose cause this evil is upon us. So they cast **lots**, and the lot fell upon Jonah. Then said they unto him, Tell us, we pray thee, for whose cause this **evil** is upon us; What is thine **occupation**? and whence comest thou? what is thy country? And of what **people** art thou? And he said unto them, I am an **Hebrew**; and I fear the LORD, the **God of heaven**, which hath made the sea and the dry **land**. Then were the men **exceedingly** afraid, and

# WORD SEARCH

```
A B I J Y L G N I D E E C X E
H A N O J U T S E P M E T A X
S S E N E V A E H F O D O G E
E I I V I J O P P A Z R I R N
S Q A R I N D U N R W O N E O
S T U T E L E N B E E L R A I
R A O I T P W V A Y R E E T T
E R B L F I E O E L B H T W A
N S R A T H M O Y H E T S I P
I H O X S S T A P T H F A N U
R I K E O L A A F L Q O M D C
A S E C H N E C L O E D P L C
M H N S T O L E N G N R I S O
S S E R A W E O P H A O H T S
P A S S E N D E K C I W S E D
```

said unto him. Why hast thou done this? For the men knew that he fled from the presence of the LORD, because he had told them.

JONAH 1:1–10

# 50

## NOAH'S DESCENDANTS

Now these are the **generations** of the **sons** of **Noah**, **Shem**, **Ham**, and **Japheth**: and unto them were sons born after the **flood**. The sons of Japheth; **Gomer**, and **Magog**, and **Madai**, and **Javan**, and **Tubal**, and **Meshech**, and **Tiras**. And the sons of Gomer; **Ashkenaz**, and **Riphath**, and **Togarmah**. And the sons of Javan; **Elishah**, and **Tarshish**, **Kittim**, and **Dodanim**. By these were the isles of the **Gentiles** divided in their **lands**; every one after his tongue, after their families, in their nations.

GENESIS 10:1–5

# WORD SEARCH

```
M A G O G C B H A H S I L E S
A J E V D H A N A E H Y V Y N
R A N B H U A S S D E B N N O
Y P T J P V D Y H S M U G M S
S H I L A N J F K V R T O E T
N E L J A C H C E H S E M K A
O T E L W A C N N E W Q E L R
I H S F F V B G A J T H R R S
T M D S A E B V Z O I Q U I H
A I O H R M L U G C R A C P I
R N O V T A D A Y I A N D H S
E A L F B H R E M B S V C A H
N D F U N M B C X R T S M T M
E O T R A R M I T T I K I H M
G D W H E G H J U H A O N N H
```

# FAITH

In this puzzle, can you find the word *faith* 35 different times? It may help to make a tally mark in the space below each time you find one.

*Verily I say unto you, If ye have faith, and doubt not, ye shall not only do this which is done to the fig tree, but also if ye shall say unto this mountain, Be thou removed, and be thou cast into the sea; it shall be done.*

MATTHEW 21:21

# WORD SEARCH

```
A  H  T  I  A  F  T  F  A  I  T  H  T  H  T
H  T  T  H  F  I  A  F  H  T  I  A  F  T  I
F  I  A  I  T  T  H  I  F  A  I  T  H  I  A
I  A  F  I  A  I  A  A  T  T  H  F  F  A  F
T  F  I  F  H  F  I  H  A  H  T  I  A  F  A
H  T  A  T  A  T  T  F  T  F  H  F  I  A  I
F  A  I  T  H  I  F  I  A  I  F  H  T  I  T
T  A  H  I  A  T  A  T  F  H  A  A  H  T  H
F  H  I  F  H  F  I  H  T  F  T  F  I  H  A
A  T  F  T  A  I  T  A  I  A  T  A  F  T  F
F  A  I  T  H  A  H  I  F  I  H  I  H  A  H
I  A  F  T  A  T  F  A  I  T  F  T  F  T  F
H  F  I  H  T  H  I  T  A  H  I  H  I  F  A
T  A  F  T  F  T  F  A  T  A  T  A  H  A  I
F  A  I  T  H  T  I  A  F  H  F  H  I  F  F
```

# HE GAVE GIFTS

But unto every one of us is given **grace** according to the **measure** of the **gift** of **Christ**. Wherefore he saith, When he **ascended** up <u>on high</u>, he led **captivity captive**, and gave gifts unto **men**. (Now that he ascended, what is it but that he also **descended first** into the **lower parts** of the **earth**? He that descended is the same also that ascended up **far** above all **heavens**, that he might fill <u>**all things**</u>.) And he gave some, **apostles**; and some, **prophets**; and some, **evangelists**; and some, **pastors** and **teachers**.

EPHESIANS 4:7–11

# WORD SEARCH

```
P R T E A C H E R S T P A C P
F I R M H E A Y E T S A P A R
H E A V E N S S W A E M R N O
T I D A P A S T O R S T H E H
S S F E E A S P L R S A T V E
T A R B D C V U C T S I R H C
S H G I H N O A R R I F A N A
I A S C F D E D N E C S E D L
L E V I T P A C W O L M O K L
E G I F T A P O S T L E S L T
G N A S C E N D F A R I F T H
N A C A P T U J A S A E M S I
A V E A R E C A R G A R G O N
V E C A P T I V I T Y A F P G
E P A S T S T E H P O R P A S
```

# fifty 53 three

## A NEW THING

**Remember** ye not the **former** things, neither **consider** the things of old. **Behold**, I will do a <u>**new thing**</u>; now it shall **spring** forth; shall ye not **know** it? I will even <u>**make a way**</u> in the **wilderness**, and **rivers** in the **desert**. The **beast** of the **field** shall **honour** me, the **dragons** and the **owls: because** I give **waters** in the wilderness, and rivers in the desert, to **give drink** to my **people**, my **chosen**.

ISAIAH 43:18–20

# WORD SEARCH

```
B I J H O N O U R G A S W R T
A M V N S K D E S E R T E C I
Y O A L I P B G I U Q D N M K
U X W K P M R H C F I P H B A
D O G S E S D I X S J U C D S
R H P M O A F E N D B E A S T
I L E D P K W O L G F S E W G
N R C E L S C A P T O N P K D
K E V G E U Y Q Y S R E V I R
C I W A T E R S Z E M A U D A
G Z O T S V M N D X E K L P G
A U N J H D B L V B R O W I O
F O K A P I I A N C H O S E N
D L E I F W N T M E S G A J S
B A D W H Y U G B E C A U S E
```

# 54

## THE THRONE IN HEAVEN

After this I looked, and, behold, a **door** was opened in **heaven**: and the first **voice** which I heard was as it were of a **trumpet** talking with me; which said, Come up hither, and I will shew thee things which must be hereafter. And immediately I was in the **spirit**: and, behold, a **throne** was set in heaven, and one sat on the throne. And he that sat was to look upon like a **jasper** and a <u>**sardine stone**</u>: and there was a **rainbow** round about the throne, in sight like unto an **emerald**. And round about the throne were **four** and **twenty** seats: and upon the **seats** I saw four and twenty **elders** sitting, clothed in **white raiment**; and they had on their heads **crowns** of **gold**. And out of the throne proceeded **lightnings** and thunderings and voices: and there were seven **lamps** of **fire** burning before the throne, which are the seven Spirits of God.

REVELATION 4:1–5

# WORD SEARCH

```
D G C T E P M U R T O M F W T
A E F J K U I R R E P S A J H
D N S S E H J A H N F Z D D E
O O P D S G N I N T H G I L A
O T M G E R B M X D R S D B V
R S A U T V O E S N W O R C E
F E L D E R S N Y T N E W T N
B N D D W T T T Y V N D O A T
E I B Q H I A C C F D F B C G
F D F E R T E V E E Y R N M O
N R R I Y U S D F R N U I B L
F A P D C X B T Y A I O A C D
N S C F N H F Y R F H F R F D
E M E R A L D D E E E T I H W
W E R D N F V O I C E E W D T
```

# HOW DRY I AM

And all the **congregation** of the **children** of Israel journeyed from the **wilderness of Sin**, after their journeys, according to the **commandment** of the LORD, and **pitched** in **Rephidim**: and there was no water for the **people** to drink. Wherefore the people did chide with **Moses**, and said, Give us water that we may **drink**. And Moses said unto them, Why chide ye with me? wherefore do ye **tempt the LORD**?  And the people thirsted there for **water**; and the people **murmured** against Moses, and said, Wherefore is this that thou hast brought us up out of **Egypt**, to kill us and our children and our **cattle** with **thirst**? And Moses cried unto the LORD, saying, What shall I do unto this people? they be almost ready to **stone me**.  And the LORD said unto Moses, Go on before the people, and take with thee of the elders of Israel; and thy **rod**, wherewith thou smotest the **river**, take in thine **hand**, and go. Behold, I will stand before thee there upon the **rock in Horeb**; and thou shalt smite the rock, and there shall come water out of it, that the people may drink. And Moses did so in the sight of the **elders of Israel**.

EXODUS 17:1–6

# WORD SEARCH

```
E N F D D Q N E R D L I H C T
L J W E E Z I G C V T N B P B
D Z E R L R S Y K L E D M N E
E X T U P E F P S F M R O O R
R C N M O M O T A G P I H R O
S M E R E E S P M H T B A I H
O O M U P N S U C A T T L E N
F S D M D O E R G M H R T U I
I E N N T T N E B C E I S Y K
S S A G R S R P O O L V R N C
R H M F E G E H S N O E I R O
A V M D N H D I T T R R H E R
E B O O W O L D O E D I T W Q
L N C S Q T I I N N L J H B G
P M R E T A W M D E H C T I P
```

# GOD SHALL BE WITH YOU

Therefore I **write** these things being **absent**, lest being **present** I should use **sharpness**, according to the **power** which the **Lord** hath given me to **edification**, and not to **destruction**. Finally, **brethren**, **farewell**. Be perfect, be of **good comfort**, be of one **mind**, live in **peace**; and the **God** of **love** and peace shall be with you. **Greet** one another with an **holy kiss**. All the **saints** salute you. The **grace** of the Lord **Jesus Christ**, and the love of God, and the **communion** of the **Holy Ghost**, be with you all. **Amen.**

2 CORINTHIANS 13:10–14

# WORD SEARCH

```
W R D E S T R U C T I O N L A
D N I M A B N O I N U M M O C
J E S U S C H R I S T R P R T
S H A R N O I T A C I F I D E
W P A B S E N T L O R I D E E
B R E L L E W E R A F T E D R
S S I K Y L O H F A S E E R G
M H P T H O P D O O G M O C R
A A A M E N S O H L O R A H S
M R P E A T C G W S P E A R P
E P W R N I Y A B E C S T C Y
G N H I K L N T A C R S B A E
L E A G O T O C O M F O R T H
O S G H M I E V T N E S E R P
H S P O W E B R E T H R E N M
```

# fifty57ven

## NOT ASHAMED

I am **ready** to **preach** the <u>**gospel to you**</u> that are at **Rome** also. <u>**For I am not**</u> **ashamed** of the **gospel** of **Christ**: for it is the <u>**power of God**</u> unto **salvation** to <u>**every one**</u> that **believeth**; to the <u>**Jew first**</u>, and also to the **Greek**. For **therein** is the **righteousness** of God **revealed** from <u>**faith to faith**</u>: as it is **written**, The **just** <u>**shall live**</u> by **faith**.

ROMANS 1:15–17

# WORD SEARCH

```
W  N  I  E  R  E  H  T  N  E  T  T  I  R  W
P  R  E  A  C  H  S  M  F  K  U  X  Y  A  Q
U  D  I  U  H  R  J  L  P  O  S  D  L  P  T
J  E  C  G  I  T  F  G  Y  I  A  D  O  S  W
O  L  Z  F  H  S  I  O  D  E  O  Z  I  A  B
S  A  W  E  M  T  T  A  R  G  C  R  S  L  E
C  E  K  A  V  L  E  B  F  I  H  H  D  V  L
J  V  O  B  E  E  K  O  N  C  A  P  U  A  I
U  E  Y  P  U  V  R  H  U  M  S  M  L  T  E
S  R  S  D  Q  E  O  Y  E  S  B  F  N  I  V
T  O  Z  L  W  I  M  D  O  D  N  U  L  O  E
G  Q  F  O  P  Y  E  P  A  N  G  E  J  N  T
L  E  P  S  O  G  X  G  R  E  E  K  S  C  H
U  H  T  I  A  F  O  T  H  T  I  A  F  S  U
S  H  A  L  L  L  I  V  E  G  P  N  I  L  K
```

# fifty**58**eight

# ISRAEL CALLED TO REPENTANCE

If thou wilt **return**, O **Israel**, saith the Lord, return unto me: and if thou wilt put away thine **abominations** out of my **sight**, then shalt thou not **remove**. And thou shalt **swear**, The Lord liveth, in **truth**, in **judgment**, and in **righteousness**; and the **nations** shall **bless** themselves in him, and in him shall they **glory**. For thus saith the Lord to the **men** of **Judah** and **Jerusalem**, Break up your fallow **ground**, and **sow** not among **thorns**. Circumcise yourselves to the **Lord**, and take away the foreskins of your **heart**, ye men of Judah and inhabitants of Jerusalem: lest my **fury** come forth like **fire**, and burn that none can **quench** it, because of the **evil** of your doings.

JEREMIAH 4:1–4

# WORD SEARCH

```
R D N M R S X T N E M G D U J
E C T J I W J Y E R V N H K O
T G E G G E E Y R U F A T Y L
U S H L H A R N B H L T F H I
R T O H T R U F N M R I L E S
N R A C E D S B Y T R O V N R
Y C D N O F A E R E R N G E A
D B G E U B L A M D V S M M E
E J R U S W E Q D W N O L B L
M U O Q N H M D V V V W A N D
R O U R E D A H G E S E O S I
V U N A S T E T H O R N S S H
E P D E S B J U D A H A S E F
E M V W N T A R D E B F F L N
T N B S N O I T A N I M O B A
```

The king shall **joy** in thy strength, O Lᴏʀᴅ; and in thy salvation how **greatly** shall he **rejoice**! Thou hast given him <u>**his heart's desire**</u>, and hast not withholden the request of his lips. Selah. For thou **preventest** him with the **blessings** of goodness: thou settest a **crown** of <u>pure gold</u> on his head. He asked **life** of thee, and thou gavest it him, even **length** of days <u>for ever and ever</u>. His glory is great in thy salvation: honour and **majesty** hast thou laid upon him. For thou hast made him most blessed for ever: thou hast made him exceeding glad with thy countenance. For the **king** trusteth in the Lᴏʀᴅ, and through the mercy of the most High he shall not be moved. Thine hand shall find out all thine **enemies**: thy right hand shall find out those that hate thee. Thou shalt make them as a **fiery** oven in the time of thine **anger**: the Lᴏʀᴅ shall **swallow** them up in his **wrath**, and the fire shall **devour** them. Their **fruit** shalt thou destroy from the earth, and their **seed** from among the children of men. For they intended evil **against** thee: they imagined a **mischievous device**, which they are not able to perform. Therefore shalt thou make them turn their back, when thou shalt make ready thine **arrows** upon thy **strings** against the face of them. Be thou exalted, Lᴏʀᴅ, in thine own strength: so will we **sing** and **praise** thy power.

# WORD SEARCH

```
N A G E L Y R E I F S B O P A
I P U R E G O L D U H L X R P
R M E I E R E J O I C E M A R
U A E S R A X C U S G S I I A
O J T E H E T T G G S S S D I
V E S D T K G L K N E I C T S
E S E S G D I N Y I I N H I E
D T T T N F E N A R M G I U S
Z Y N R E W P E G T E S E R W
W I E A L J O V S S N M V F O
R E V E D N A R E V E R O F R
A G E H C H I O C E K L U N R
T N R S I A W O L L A W S W A
H I P I D E V I C E X E R H J
T S O H T S N I A G A L J N M
```

# COUNT ON ETERNAL LIFE

Below are scripture passages related to eternal life. Your challenge is to find the *numbers* in the passage. If the scripture is John 3:16–17, you will find 31617 in the grid.

Job **19:26–27**

Psalm **16:10–11**

Isaiah **26:18–19**

Matthew **19:15–17**

Mark **10:17–18**

Luke **20:35–36**

John **3:16–17**

John **5:28–29**

John **6:39–40**

John **6:47–48**

John **6:53–54**

John **10:27–28**

John **11:25–26**

Acts **13:47–48**

Romans **6:22–23**

Romans **8:10–11**

1 Corinthians **15:20–23**

1 Corinthians **15:42–46**

1 Corinthians **15:51–54**

1 Thessalonians **4:16–17**

1 John **2:24–25**

1 John **5:11–13**

Jude **1:20–21**

Revelation **7:15–17**

# WORD SEARCH

```
3 9 8 7 2 4 9 1 8 2 7 2 0 1 2
7 1 5 1 9 1 3 5 8 0 1 9 7 7 3
9 7 6 7 8 0 0 4 1 3 3 2 2 2 6
0 8 4 1 6 9 7 1 0 4 6 8 0 5 3
1 5 6 8 7 4 1 3 7 5 7 2 9 2 6
3 2 4 5 6 2 7 0 2 1 5 7 1 8 1
4 1 9 0 3 5 9 4 3 1 8 6 0 2 5
7 1 5 1 7 8 5 2 4 2 2 5 8 9 8
4 0 1 9 8 3 9 8 7 5 0 7 9 1 7
8 1 4 2 5 4 1 3 4 2 8 3 2 4 4
5 8 3 6 7 3 1 5 6 6 7 4 5 5 9
0 4 1 2 5 2 0 9 7 3 0 6 1 3 0
1 9 6 7 1 6 1 4 1 4 9 5 2 5 6
4 3 5 0 9 8 6 0 2 3 5 4 1 6 7
2 6 4 2 4 5 1 4 8 1 0 7 0 9 8
```

Arise

Bier

City

Compassion

<u>Dead Man</u>

Disciples

Gate

Glorified

God

Judaea

Lord

Mother

Nain

<u>Only Son</u>

Region

Speak

Touched

<u>Weep Not</u>

Widow

# WORD SEARCH

```
D J O N L Y S O N B O I G E R
I U W E L A R I I I A D U J R
S D C I T O R E Q A G A T E I
C A D I S C R O N L R C G O R
I E A R N B I D A R N I A N O
W A S P E A K U O T O T S D L
C E A R I S M S P N E Y J E G
O R E H T O M D W Q S C U O T
M C I P L O R W A E P S A E D
P A R I N D W S D E H C U O T
A M O T H O W E E N D A D U J
S G L O D I T K L P I C S I D
G O D I I N O I S S A P M O C
A R W S G L O R I F I E D S E
T O U C H S E L P I C S I D W
```

# sixty two

# THE TREE OF LIFE

And he **shewed** me a **<u>pure river</u>** of **water** of life, **clear** as **crystal**, proceeding out of the **throne** of **God** and of the **Lamb**. In the **midst** of the **street** of it, and on **<u>either side</u>** of the river, was there the **<u>tree of life</u>**, which **bare twelve** manner of **fruits**, and **yielded** her fruit every **month**: and the **leaves** of the tree were for the **healing** of the **nations**.

REVELATION 22:1–2

# WORD SEARCH

```
O F R U I T S H I E L M I D S
C L O N G O R A E L C R E A N
S E V A E L S E C R Y S I N O
T R S D O W N H E I V B R E I
L A T S Y R C E I O T M O R T
I M R P A T N A T S F A M A A
G A E N H W D L H I G L T B N
P H E A K E U I E T R A I G H
M L T I W L F N R Y N C K F R
O A N E R V E G S H D O G A E
N T H C L E M B I L A W M I T
B S L A K R C H D S T T L R A
H D Y R E V I R E R U P Q U W
Y I E L D E D O N T H R O N E
O M I S T H A W E D G O T I B
```

# GOD IS. . . (PART 1)

A **Consuming Fire** (Deuteronomy 4:24)

A **Jealous God** (Deuteronomy 6:15)

**Among You** (Joshua 3:10)

**Angry** with the wicked (Psalm 7:11)

**God of Gods** (Deuteronomy 10:17)

**Gracious** and **Merciful** (2 Chronicles 30:9)

**Great** (Job 36:26)

**Greater Than Man** (Job 33:12)

**In All Things** (Deuteronomy 4:7)

In the **Generation** of the **Righteous** (Psalm 14:5)

**Mighty** (Job 36:5)

My Strength and **Power** (2 Samuel 22:33)

**Not a Man** (Numbers 23:19)

**One Lord** (Deuteronomy 6:4)

Our Refuge and **Strength** (Psalm 46:1)

The **King** of All the Earth (Psalm 47:7)

Thy **Refuge** (Deuteronomy 33:27)

**With Thee** (Genesis 21:22)

**Witness** (Genesis 31:50)

# WORD SEARCH

```
C W I N A M A T O N S T L P N
A O T C O D A A J C G O K G A
N N N E F C T E O O N L R M
D E H S R A H P A Z D S U A N
Y L A G U E E U L X O U F C A
E O C N M M M K O V F O I I H
E R S I E R I O U E G E C O T
H D T H A N G N S G O T R U R
T Y R T G B H S G U D H E S E
H D E L T S T E O F S G M N T
T U N L B L Y S D E I I H U A
I O G A A P O W E R O R G T E
W I T N E S S E R M B W E S R
I L H I L N O I T A R E N E G
P C A U O Y G N O M A N G R Y
```

# ELIJAH STAYS WITH A WIDOW WOMAN

And the word of the Lord came unto him, saying, Arise, get thee to **Zarephath**, which belongeth to **Zidon**, and **dwell** there: **behold**, I have commanded **a widow woman** there to **sustain** thee. So he arose and went to Zarephath. And when he came to the **gate** of the city, behold, the widow woman was there **gathering** of **sticks**: and he called to her, and said, **Fetch** me, I pray thee, **a little water** in a **vessel**, that I may **drink**. And as she was going to fetch it, he called to her, and said, Bring me, I pray thee, a **morsel** of **bread** in thine hand. And she said, As the Lord thy God liveth, I have not a **cake**, but an **handful** of **meal** in a barrel, and a little oil in a cruse: and, behold, I am gathering two sticks, that I may go in and **dress** it for me and **my son**, that we may eat it, and die. And Elijah said unto her, **Fear not**; go and do as thou hast said: but make me **thereof** a little cake first, and bring it unto me, and after make for thee and for thy son. For thus saith the Lord God of Israel, The **barrel** of meal shall not **waste**, neither shall the **cruse of oil** fail, until the day that the Lord sendeth **rain** upon the earth. And she went and did **according** to the saying of **Elijah**: and she, and he, and her house, did eat many days.

1 Kings 17:8–15

# WORD SEARCH

```
L A E M H A J I L E S N E W I
B E H O L D E N C K I E X E L
E V T R F N B O C A V D K C A
X G A S U E O I T R E R N A C
U N H E I U T S T N S E C U C
N I P L Q S U C Y A S S R D O
I R E P H S A Z H M E S U A R
A E R L E R R A B O L O S E D
R H A L I T T L E W A T E R I
T T Z S G O L L E W D H O B N
I A E I N A Z O U O R A F L G
H G Y R D N T J M D I H O Y B
G Y A F E O K E E I N P I H E
O E L U F D N A H W K Z L G L
F O E R E H T H C A E T S A W
```

# FIVE CROSSES #2

In this puzzle, you will find five-letter words that are commonly found in the Bible. Your search will be aided by the fact that each word has a partner word that crosses its center, forming either an "x" or a "+" shape.

| | |
|---|---|
| Bones | Satan |
| Cover | Share |
| Field | Shine |
| Found | Skull |
| Gates | Sower |
| Grass | Swear |
| Hates | Taste |
| Idols | Trust |
| Kings | Unite |
| Laugh | Utter |
| Lowly | Visit |
| Marry | Waste |
| Mourn | Wives |
| Music | World |
| Proud | Youth |

# WORD SEARCH

```
H B S N U L M O E P S T W Q G
O A E T K N J N U L K H Y R A
S A T A N S I Y X B V O A J L
Y E A E G H G T O E I S D R Z
R K G Y S W D N E T S A T F E
N Z D U B A E H I Z I H C G P
I M L C I S U M G K T D V R D
Y R R A M T S X S U M J O S I
B L O E Y E G M O Y A U H L U
I D W L V D S Y N R D L L C S
P N S I Y O L K R L O D P N T
M K W B N L C E A I L N R B R
D L E I F M W Q W T S U R T E
T U A U Z O Y O X R O O K N Z
Y A R P S A F C L M D F I S M
```

*six* **66** *six*

# AS HE PURPOSETH

But this I say, He which **soweth sparingly** shall **reap** also sparingly; and he which soweth **bountifully** shall reap also bountifully. Every **man according** as he **purposeth** in his **heart**, so let him **give**; not **grudgingly**, or of **necessity**: for **God loveth** a **cheerful** giver. And God is able to make all **grace abound** toward you; that ye, always having all **sufficiency** in <u>all things</u>, may abound to **every good work**.

2 CORINTHIANS 9:6–8

# WORD SEARCH

```
G S O P A W R E A I T N U O B
R M A U O S P A R I N G L Y P
U A C R D G R A C E E H C H U
D L K P G N N H L O V E H G Y
G I A O R I E T U S D H E R T
I V L S U H C E S N L A E A I
N E T E D T D W U T H I R A S
G V E T G L S O W E J H F B S
L E R H M L B S G N T S U O E
Y R O K Y A T R A E H P L U C
W G W R S U N S V O B A W D E
P I E N E C E O R O W R G O N
A V W O Y L L U F I T N U O B
E E S U F F I C I E N C Y G E
R E A T H G N I D R O C C A R
```

# LIVE RIGHT

Let love be without **dissimulation. Abhor** that which is evil; **cleave** to that <u>**which is good**</u>. Be kindly **affectioned** one to another with <u>**brotherly love**</u>; in **honour** preferring one another; <u>**not slothful**</u> in business; **fervent** in spirit; **serving** the Lord; **rejoicing** in hope; **patient** in **tribulation**; continuing <u>**instant in prayer**</u>; **distributing** to the necessity of saints; given to **hospitality.** <u>**Bless them**</u> which **persecute** you: bless, and <u>**curse not**</u>. Rejoice with them that do rejoice, and <u>**weep with them**</u> that weep. Be of the same mind one toward another. Mind not high things, but condescend to men of low estate. Be not wise in your <u>**own conceits**</u>. Recompense to no man evil for evil. Provide things **honest** in the sight of all men.

ROMANS 12:9–17

# WORD SEARCH

```
P E R S E C U T E C V B N M G
Z I E A L U F H T O L S T O N
D U Y G D G E O Y B Q U N M I
E T A N O N V N T R X O O E C
N B R I O I A E I O I W I H I
O L P T G V E S L T Z N T T O
I E N U S R L T A H C C A H J
T S I B I E C L T E T O L T E
C S T I H S U S I R N N U I R
E T N R C M R D P L E C B W R
F H A T I R S F S Y I E I P U
F E T S H O E G O L T I R E O
A M S I W H N H H O A T T E N
R I N D Q B O J L V P S P W O
D E I W U A T T N E V R E F H
```

# A BEND IN THE RIVER

No waterways are completely straight. Be sure to follow the turns these rivers and brooks mentioned in the Bible take. It wouldn't do for you to go off course. In this puzzle, each hidden word will bend at an angle instead of appearing in one straight line.

**Abana** (2 Kings 5:12)

**Ahava** (Ezra 8:21)

**Arnon** (Deuteronomy 4:48)

**Besor** (1 Samuel 30:9)

**Cedron** (John 18:1)

**Chebar** (Ezekiel 1:1)

**Cherith** (1 Kings 17:3)

**Egypt** (Genesis 15:18)

**Eshcol** (Numbers 13:24)

**Euphrates** (Genesis 2:14)

**Gaash** (1 Chronicles 11:32)

**Gad** (2 Samuel 24:5)

**Gihon** (Genesis 2:13)

**Gozan** (2 Kings 17:6)

**Hiddekel** (Genesis 2:14)

**Jabbok** (Deuteronomy 2:37)

**Jordan** (Mark 1:5)

**Kanah** (Joshua 16:8)

**Kidron** (2 Samuel 15:23)

**Kishon** (Judges 4:7)

**Pharpar** (2 Kings 5:12)

**Pison** (Genesis 2:11)

**Ulai** (Daniel 8:2)

**Zered** (Deuteronomy 2:13)

# WORD SEARCH

```
R D A N U A T E S O H Z C E D
X O Y I R B U L A G A E I Q R
U S J H G S H E I X H P B U O
L G P N O N D R K C D H I A N
K U K R X D A P U E V S O W R
E S I A I P W A N A L A H A N
J W S H Z R K B Y Z G A F W A
B K H O N A P A J X N P Z Y K
E G Y E J H O I E O A S E B S
X U R P I P U C S D O N A U N
A H A V T D E V H R J R E D O
K L K A B S F Y T L E X P I R
O U O J H G L U I Z K J Q D G
B I E C G Z O E R E H C I W I
B A J W A D Q Z A N U K N O H
```

There were **present** at that **season** some that <u>told him</u> of the **Galilaeans**, whose **blood Pilate** had **mingled** with their **sacrifices**. And **Jesus answering** said unto them, **Suppose** ye that these Galilaeans were **sinners above** all the Galilaeans, because they **suffered** <u>such things</u>? <u>**I tell you**</u>, Nay: but, **except** ye **repent**, ye shall all likewise **perish**. Or those **eighteen**, upon whom the <u>**tower in Siloam fell**</u>, and <u>**slew them**</u>, **think** ye that they were sinners above all men that **dwelt** in **Jerusalem**? I tell you, **Nay:** but, except ye repent, ye shall all **likewise** perish.

LUKE 13:1–5

Secret message:

\_\_\_\_\_ \_\_\_\_\_ \_\_\_\_\_ _____ \_\_\_\_\_ \_\_\_\_\_

_____ \_\_\_ \_\_\_\_\_ \_\_\_\_ _____?

# WORD SEARCH

```
E E F O R S N A E A L I L A G
W I T P E C X E H S A L T O N
T T G A H M E S I R O F E E I
A T O H L U I N U R E P D F R
S T W W T I N N A S S W P S E
E E O T E E P A G H E E R U W
C P A L R R E N Y L V J E F S
I E I S D E I N T L E L S F N
F R A G O H V N R E O D E E A
I I F S T N I O S E I L N R O
R S A H M W E M B I P L T E B
C H C L J E R U S A L E M D L
A U E S I W E K I L K O N N O
S I T E L L Y O U O W N A T O
K N I H T X S L E W T H E M D
```

# WALK BY FAITH

Therefore we are always **confident**, knowing that, whilst we are at **home** in the **body**, we are **absent** from the **Lord**: (for we **walk** by **faith**, not by **sight**:) we are confident, I say, and **willing** rather to be absent from the body, and to be **present** with the Lord. Wherefore we **labour**, that, whether present or absent, we may be **accepted** of him. For we must all **appear** before the <u>**judgment seat**</u> of **Christ**; that every one may **receive** the things **done** in his body, **according** to that he <u>**hath done**</u>, whether it be **good** or **bad**.

2 CORINTHIANS 5:6–10

# WORD SEARCH

```
L D E T P E C C A C F B M O H
F O P R E S E N T A S O B A Y
A T R W I L L I I D P D L D A
I S N D A P H T U J A D O O G
H I A E D O H A N E E B O B N
G R P H D S L E T A N C A E I
I H P O S I A S F H O H B V D
S C E M A S F T A L D R S I R
L L A K E I C N I O R O E E O
A O R A T G O E O R E A N C C
B R T H G I S M W C C P T E C
O F O L L I W G A W E P D R A
U J U D G M R D L X I E C I A
R D O N H A T U K B V A O O G
E M O H E R P J W I L L I N G
```

# SNOW WHITE

And **Miriam** and Aaron spake against **Moses** because of the **Ethiopian woman** whom he had married: for he had **married** an Ethiopian woman. And they said, Hath the Lord indeed spoken only by Moses? hath he not spoken also by us? And the Lord heard it. . . . And **the Lord** came down in the **pillar** of the cloud, and stood in the door of the **tabernacle**, and called **Aaron** and Miriam: and they both came forth. And he said, Hear now **my words**: If there be a **prophet** among you, I the Lord will make myself known unto him in a **vision**, and will speak unto him in a **dream**. My **servant** Moses is not so, who is **faithful** in all mine house. With him will I speak **mouth to mouth**, even apparently, and not in **dark speeches**; and the **similitude** of the Lord shall he behold: wherefore then were ye not afraid to speak against my servant Moses? And the **anger** of the Lord was **kindled** against them; and he departed. And the **cloud** departed from off the tabernacle; and, behold, Miriam became leprous, **white as snow**: and Aaron looked upon Miriam, and, behold, she was **leprous**.

Numbers 12:1–2, 5–10

# WORD SEARCH

```
P I L L A R D E L D N I K H E
R B V T M R E G N A Z X V T N
O S D H F X J P R R P S H U M
P D R E A M K O E K R I K O K
H R E L I A L I W S O M I M L
E O L O T R R U Q P N I Y O P
T W C R H Z R O I E T L A T U
S Y A D F M G A N E O I M H S
U M N X U N N N M C S T R T E
O M R J L W F O I H D U E U R
R N E H O P S I R E U D H O V
P F B M I E T S I S O E T M A
E K A U S A Y I A Q L V O O N
L N T P M L U V M A C Z M Y T
F D C Q W O N S S A E T I H W
```

# RUTH AND BOAZ MARRY

So **Boaz** took **Ruth**, and she was his **wife**: and when he went in unto her, the LORD gave her conception, and she **bare a son**. And the **women** said unto **Naomi**, Blessed be the LORD, which hath not left thee this day without a **kinsman**, that his name may be **famous** in Israel. And he shall be unto thee a **restorer** of thy **life**, and a **nourisher** of thine **old age**: for thy **daughter** in law, which **loveth** thee, which is better to thee than **seven sons**, hath born him. And Naomi took the **child**, and laid it in her bosom, and became **nurse** unto it. And the women her **neighbours** gave it a name, saying, There is a son born to Naomi; and they called his name **Obed**: he is the **father** of **Jesse**, the father of **David**.

RUTH 4:13–17

# WORD SEARCH

```
B D B T Y U C J B N E M O W C
A D A U G H T E R Z F D F K S
R E D D S J B S U I I E I A R
E B B Y R S G S J K L N D U P
A O D N U E Z E B D S T T L C
S B D O O V A E Q M Z H G H H
O C M U B E X V A F D L I R K
N A V R H N F N N B O L E E G
F Y J I G S J I H V D N B R I
V E D S I O N E E G A D L O M
E A I H E N Y T K S S C G T O
B Z V E N S H D F I D B A S A
W A A R N U R S E F F U B E N
D O D Q H O A U F A T H E R Y
D B X G L F E I H C D E F I W
```

# GOD IS. . . (PART 2)

A **Sun and Shield** (Psalm 84:11)

**Faithful** (1 Corinthians 10:13)

**For Me** (Psalm 56:9)

**Good to Israel** (Psalm 73:1)

**Holy** (Psalm 99:9)

**In the Heavens** (Psalm 115:3)

**Judge** (Psalm 50:6)

**Light** (1 John 1:5)

**Love** (1 John 4:8)

**Mine Helper** (Psalm 54:4)

**My Defence** (Psalm 59:17)

My **King of Old** (Psalm 74:12)

**My Salvation** (Isaiah 12:2)

No **Respecter** of Persons (Acts 10:34)

**Not Mocked** (Galatians 6:7)

**Righteous** in all his works (Daniel 9:14)

The Rock of **My Refuge** (Psalm 94:22)

**True** (John 3:33)

**With Us** (Isaiah 8:10)

# WORD SEARCH

```
G R E P L E H E N I M J I H M
F D S A Q P G V L W Q I P L Y
H T R D E K C O M T O N K E S
J H E Y M V I L J A I T T A A
K O W U R E K L H L R H F R L
L L Q I O U I O G U R E B S V
M Y D E F E N C E F I H X I A
W E D I V M G K E H G E E O T
A I F O C A O E P T H A G T I
T W T P X I F D T I T V U D O
E H J H Z F O G R A E E F O N
G A G K U L L P T F O N E O D
D L E I H S D N A N U S R G C
U W U Y L A I P N V S Q Y F B
J S J R E T C E P S E R M E A
```

# NUMBER THE STARS

Praise ye the LORD: for it is **good** to <u>**sing praises**</u> unto <u>**our God**</u>; for it is **pleasant**; and praise is comely. The LORD doth <u>**build up**</u> Jerusalem: he **gathereth** together the **outcasts** of **Israel**. He **healeth** the **broken** in **heart**, and <u>**bindeth up**</u> their **wounds**. He telleth the **number** of the **stars**; he **calleth** them all by their **names**. Great is our Lord, and of <u>**great power**</u>: his **understanding** is infinite. The LORD <u>**lifteth up**</u> the **meek**: he casteth the **wicked** down to the ground. Sing unto the LORD with **thanksgiving**; sing praise upon the **harp** unto our God.

PSALM 147:1–7

# WORD SEARCH

```
B E L H A T G D H T E L A E H
S H A L Y O N A M E S O A R P
T R G N O R E B M U N L Q U C
P U N D E R S T A N D I N G A L
L B I N D E T H U P R F D A L
I R V U O T W O L L E T E T L
S O I P G I R Z M P W E K H E
T K G D R O L A U T O T C E T
S E S L U M I D E G P H I R H
A N K A O N L R I H T U W E S
C I N T G I M E E K A P M T T
T J A C U K I S R A E L G H A
U F H B M E L A S U R E J F R
O U T S E S I A R P G N I S S
K P L E A S A N T S D N U O W
```

Then the LORD answered **Job** out of the **whirlwind**, and said, <u>**Who is this**</u> that **darkeneth counsel** by **words** without knowledge? <u>**Gird up**</u> now <u>**thy loins**</u> like a man; for I will **demand** of thee, and <u>**answer thou me**</u>. <u>**Where wast thou**</u> when I laid the **foundations** of the **earth**? **Declare**, if thou hast **understanding**. Who hath **laid** the measures thereof, if thou knowest? Or who hath **stretched** <u>**the line**</u> upon it? **Whereupon** are the foundations thereof fastened? Or who laid the <u>**corner stone**</u> thereof; when the <u>**morning stars**</u> sang **together**, and all the <u>**sons of God**</u> shouted for joy?

JOB 38:1–7

*Secret message:*

_____ \_\_\_\_\_ _____ \_\_\_\_\_ _____
\_\_\_\_ _____ _____ \_\_\_\_ _____?

# WORD SEARCH

```
U W H I W H I R L W I N D C D
N W H T W H O C O O N S T S A
D E H L S L E A T R I O N N R
E S S E A O P R E D R E S O K
R R M E R U N H E S I W N I E
S A T E D E T S N U E A I T N
T T O R R E W I O R P N L A E
A S I J G A O A T F E O D D T
N G I O N L L H S H G T N N H
D N T B Y E O C R T E O H U D
I I I H S U R S E C T L D O N
N N T N M H D A N D P H I F A
G R U E T E E A R T H R O N M
O O S I H T S I O H W F J U E
C M O S T R E T C H E D B X D
```

# ESTHER REVEALS HAMAN'S PLOT

So the **king** and **Haman** came to banquet with Esther the **queen**. And the king said again unto **Esther** on the second day at the **banquet** of wine, What is thy **petition**, queen Esther? and it shall be **granted** thee: and what is thy **request**? and it shall be performed, even to the half of the **kingdom**. Then Esther the queen answered and said, If I have found **favour** in thy sight, O king, and if it **please** the king, let my life be given me at my petition, and **my people** at my request: For we are **sold**, I and my people, to be **destroyed**, to be **slain**, and to **perish**. But if we had been sold for **bondmen** and bondwomen, I had held my **tongue**, although the **enemy** could not countervail the king's damage. Then the king **Ahasuerus** answered and said unto Esther the queen, Who is he, and where is he, that durst presume in his **heart** to do so? And Esther said, The adversary and enemy is this wicked Haman. Then Haman was **afraid** before the king and the queen.

ESTHER 7:1–6

# WORD SEARCH

```
A C H B P E R I S H H O I Q Y
H A M A N N N L K F A V O U R
A J K N M I D E Y O R T S E D
S F B Q G A N E M W V G Q E N
U K F U D L V M W Y Q U S N O
E P L E A S E I J H E D F E I
R S X T R O B N D S A E J L T
U F S N F L M G T W R U I P I
S F Y G U D O G S E U G N O T
G R A N T E D R W D T U S E E
Q E E Q N Y G D A I E H K P P
D H N E M D N O B A G R L Y Q
C T B C E A I B S R J N F M F
N S I T R D K N G F E D I N C
U E O N J C J T R A E H C K N
```

# COUNT ON HOSPITALITY

Below are scripture passages related to being hospitable. Your challenge is to find the *numbers* in the passage. If the scripture is John 3:16–17, you will find 31617 in the grid.

Genesis **12:15–16**

Genesis **14:17–18**

Genesis **19:1–11**

Genesis **24:31–32**

Genesis **29:13–14**

Genesis **45:16–20**

Exodus **22:21–22**

Joshua **2:1, 15–16**

Leviticus **19:9–10**

Leviticus **19:33–34**

1 Kings **17:10–24**

Matthew **25:35–40**

Mark **9:41–42**

Luke **10:38–39**

Luke **14:7–11**

Luke **19:1–10**

Acts **16:14–15**

Acts **20:34–35**

Romans **12:10–18**

2 Corinthians **8:13–14**

James **2:15–16**

1 John **3:16–17**

# WORD SEARCH

```
9 8 2 8 4 7 6 4 5 1 0 5 3 1 0
6 7 0 1 4 1 3 1 9 2 4 7 6 4 1
4 3 3 3 9 1 2 4 6 4 8 1 5 9 8
5 1 4 8 6 3 0 1 1 9 0 3 7 0 7
8 0 3 1 7 2 5 9 5 0 5 7 0 1 9
3 2 5 9 8 4 7 1 1 2 3 8 1 3 8
7 1 6 1 3 6 1 6 1 6 2 0 9 4 1
2 8 4 3 5 1 4 1 2 4 5 2 9 5 7
0 7 3 6 9 0 7 5 1 1 7 4 1 6 1
2 9 2 1 8 5 6 1 9 6 8 6 3 2 0
8 4 1 0 2 4 3 2 3 0 1 9 5 7 2
7 9 3 4 3 1 9 1 6 0 2 4 2 8 4
6 0 1 1 5 6 0 9 3 8 3 0 1 9 0
3 4 6 7 3 7 8 1 5 4 6 8 7 5 8
9 2 3 9 0 2 9 7 8 0 1 1 9 1 6
```

# TRADITIONS AND COMMANDMENTS

Then came to **Jesus scribes** and **Pharisees**, which were of Jerusalem, saying, Why do thy **disciples** transgress the **tradition** of the elders? for they **wash** not their **hands** when they <u>eat bread</u>. But he answered and said unto them, Why do ye also **transgress** the **commandment** of God by your tradition? For God commanded, saying, **Honour** thy father and mother: and, He that curseth father or mother, let him **die** the death. But ye say, Whosoever shall say to his father or his mother, It is a **gift**, by whatsoever thou **mightest** be profited by me; and honour not his father or his mother, he shall be free. Thus have ye made the commandment of God of none **effect** by your tradition. Ye **hypocrites**, well did **Esaias prophesy** of you, saying, This people draweth nigh unto me with their **mouth**, and honoureth me with their **lips**; but their heart is **far** from me. But in **vain** they do **worship** me, teaching for **doctrines** the commandments of men.

MATTHEW 15:1–9

# WORD SEARCH

```
B T N E M D N A M M O C E G J
C F G S E T I R C O P Y H E F
H I D N I A V K H E D H S A W
S G D O C T R I N E S U R C T
C S G T Y J H P I H S R O W R
R A M I G H T E S T H B M E A
I I F F A E R E A T B R E A D
B A X C F D A Y S P I L Q W I
E S N M F W N M S E F F E C T
S E L P I C S I D E T R I Y I
D B D H Z A G T E I H M J H O
N Q R T R U R N E A E P R F N
A D V U W T E V X A C R O N J
H O N O U R S U C C B T U R I
N A S M P I S E E S I R A H P
```

# OH, PROMISE ME

Then **king David** answered and said, Call me **Bathsheba**. And she came into the king's presence, and stood before the king. And the king sware, and said, As the LORD liveth, that hath **redeemed** my soul out of **all distress**, even as I **sware** unto thee by the **LORD God of Israel**, saying, Assuredly **Solomon** thy son shall reign after me, and he shall sit upon **my throne** in my stead; even so will I certainly do this day. Then Bathsheba **bowed** with her face to the earth, and did reverence to the king, and said, Let my lord king David live for ever. And king David said, Call me **Zadok** the **priest**, and **Nathan** the **prophet**, and **Benaiah** the **son of Jehoiada**. And they came before the king. The king also said unto them, Take with you the servants of your lord, and cause Solomon my son to ride upon mine **own mule**, and bring him down to **Gihon**: and let Zadok the priest and Nathan the prophet **anoint him** there king over Israel: and blow ye with the **trumpet**, and say, God save king Solomon. Then ye shall come up after him, that he may come and sit upon my throne; for he shall be king in my stead: and I have **appointed** him to be **ruler** over Israel and over **Judah**.

1 KINGS 1:28–35

# WORD SEARCH

```
N O M O L O S A S D E F G H L
T V B P N M S D P F G R K L E
E Z X Y C V P B T T U Q A W A
P I O I B U T Y S L A T R W R
M K A D A I O H E J F O N O S
U L N E T H N R I Z X V E D I
R N O T H A M J R D N L B I F
T A I N S I Y F P E U Y T V O
O T N I H A T D Q M W Z E A D
H H T O E N H E N E C A H D O
A A H P B E R W O E F D P G G
D N I P A B O O H D J O O N D
U I M A S J N B I E K K R I R
J K U F M Z E X G R L Q P K O
E V A L L D I S T R E S S T L
```

# THE DEATH OF KING DAVID

Now the **days of David** drew **nigh** that he should die; and he charged **Solomon** his son, saying, I go the way of all the earth: be thou **strong** therefore, and shew **thyself** a man; and keep the **charge** of the LORD thy God, to walk in his ways, to keep his **statutes**, and his **commandments**, and his **judgments**, and his **testimonies**, as it is written in the **law of Moses**, that thou **mayest prosper** in all that thou doest, and whithersoever thou **turnest** thyself: that the LORD may continue his word which he **spake** concerning me, saying, If thy children take **heed** to their way, to **walk** before me in truth with all their **heart** and with all their **soul**, there shall not **fail** thee (said he) a man on the **throne** of Israel. . . . So David **slept** with his **fathers**, and was **buried** in the **city** of David.

1 KINGS 2:1–4, 10

# WORD SEARCH

```
D C A M O O N D N P O U H G T
N A J I S T S U O R E E H Y S
V I Y T E S T I M O N I E S E
D A G S S O N T O S D Q A T Y
S E P H O X E U L P E U R N A
E X E C M F M E O E I A T E M
E S I H F I D B S R R F S M N
W T B C O X N A L K U F O G U
A A D O W E A H V U B L U D D
L T L J A D M G C I O E T U E
I U E K L Y M C N U D S P J K
A T C O M M O L I O G Y E E A
F E G R A H C Y S T R H L L P
G S H T U R N E S T Y T S K S
E N O R H T F A T H E R S O T
```

# ANNOUNCEMENT TO MARY
## (LUKE 1:26–38)

Angel

Be It unto Me

Blessed

Conceive

Fear Not

Galilee

God

Highest

Highly Favoured

Holy Ghost

Jesus

Joseph

Mary

Nazareth

Power

Salutation

Son of God

Throne

Troubled

# WORD SEARCH

```
H I G T F E B L J E A N M G A
D J O S E P H W E L I L A G N
E A T D E L B U O R T L A N G
R P C H S H I T B O I A T O H
U J O N R U T R O L A N D C I
O O N W A O S Y E N E G Q O G
V S C H E Z N E R E R S T N H
A E E T G R L E J A B A S C J
F P I E N S E P O W M U E E E
Y O V R A E G H G Y L O H F D
L L E A S O N O F G O D G H T
H H A Z A N A S A L U I I L B
G G S A L U T A T I O N H N A
I I M N Y T S O H G Y L O H S
H H B E I T U N T O M E S O J
```

# THE PURPOSE OF PARABLES

And he said unto them, Know ye not this **parable**? and how then will ye know all parables? The **sower** soweth the word. And these are they by the **way side**, where the **word** is **sown**; but when they have heard, **Satan** cometh immediately, and taketh away the word that was sown in their **hearts**. And these are they likewise which are sown on **stony ground**; who, when they have heard the word, immediately **receive** it with **gladness**; and have **no root** in themselves, and so **endure** but for a time: afterward, when **affliction** or **persecution** ariseth for the word's sake, immediately they are **offended**. And these are they which are sown among **thorns**; such as hear the word, and the cares of this world, and the **deceitfulness** of **riches**, and the **lusts** of other things entering in, choke the word, and it becometh **unfruitful**. And these are they which are sown on good ground; such as hear the word, and receive it, and bring forth **fruit**, some thirtyfold, some sixty, and some an hundred.

MARK 4:13–20

# WORD SEARCH

```
D C U N F R U I T F U L Y   I G
B S T R A E H E D I S Y A W D
X O T Y F J T N A S E T E D Z
D W X V F R E G N S C B R Y N
S N N C L S N R N E D D U P D
Z C V M I E O Y O N S Z D A N
E E D S C H H F I L G T N R U
V Y E R T C T G T U H I E A O
I N D G I I G L U F J U I B R
E O N U O R I A C T K R U L G
C R E H N R J D E I N F I E Y
E O F J E J K N S E U A T H N
R O F W O R D E R C U H T W O
S T O F E E T S E E T P R A T
B S F S W V N S P D L U S T S
```

# EVERY THOUGHT CAPTIVE

For though we **walk** in the **flesh**, we <u>**do not war**</u> after the flesh: (for the **weapons** of our warfare are not **carnal**, but **mighty** through God to the <u>**pulling down**</u> of <u>**strong holds**</u>;) **casting down imaginations**, and every <u>**high thing**</u> that **exalteth** itself against the **knowledge** of God, and bringing into **captivity** every **thought** to the **obedience** of **Christ**; and **having** in a **readiness** to **revenge** all disobedience, when **your** obedience is **fulfilled**.

2 Corinthians 10:3–6

Secret message:

\_\_\_\_\_ _____ _____ _____ _____ _____

_____ \_\_\_\_\_ \_\_\_\_ _____ \_\_\_\_\_

_____ _____?

# WORD SEARCH

```
H W H I I W C S E L F H E R X
P I E R M T A H T E T L A X E
A P G W O A S L T L C W E D P
W R O H E Y G T K A T E O U D
O S W O T A N I P O G W L T R
F H T H B H P T N I N L S P E
O U G R W E I O K A I E R F A
T I L U O V D N N N T L B I D
M H T F I N O I G S S I O E I
F A O T I W G D E I A N O G N
S V Y U L L O H T N C R U N E
C I Y E G W L T O I C O N E S
F N D O N H O E R L G E O V S
D G L Y U L T I D V D I N E G
E X L A N R A C H R I S T R X
```

# FIVE CROSSES #3

In this puzzle, you will find five-letter words that are commonly found in the Bible. Your search will be aided by the fact that each word has a partner word that crosses its center, forming either an "x" or a "+" shape.

| | |
|---|---|
| Anger | Heals |
| Arrow | Heard |
| Beast | Honor |
| Begat | Learn |
| Blind | Mercy |
| Count | Money |
| Crown | Spare |
| Devil | Staff |
| Eagle | Think |
| Elder | Voice |
| Enemy | Walls |
| Exalt | Weigh |
| False | Wheat |
| Favor | Widow |
| Fight | Wound |
| Flock | Years |

# WORD SEARCH

```
S D L O Z I H U F X Y T H A F
X T Q W T D S D S D H R W J S
G A H E N H J P E E O Q O I K
W E C I O V F G A V Y C R E M
Q K L G N A L L A R I E R T Z
E B A H W K S F T N E L A X O
D L X I T O L W D T H G I F U
F N D N E S L A F J E A N G Q
I O U E H Z A G M B B E W A H
W O G O R O W O H N F L O C K
C D F E W H N B S D T K R T E
L Z F S X E E O Y R I A C N O
S R A E Y A J N R A E L E S G
W H T K S Q L X H E Z M I H A
Y G S T D U F T A H Y K S D W
```

# SMELLS IN THE BIBLE

**Aloes** (Psalm 45:8)

**Battle** (Job 39:25)

**Burnt Offering** (Genesis 8:20–21)

**Camps** (Amos 4:10)

**Cassia** (Psalm 45:8)

**Dead Fish** (Exodus 7:21)

**Dead Flies** (Ecclesiastes 10:1)

**Egypt** (Exodus 8:7–14)

**Fire** (Daniel 3:27)

**Garments** (Song of Solomon 4:11)

**Incense** (Exodus 30:7)

**Mandrakes** (Song of Solomon 7:13)

**Manna** (Exodus 16:15–20)

**Myrrh** (Psalm 45:8)

**Ointment** (John 12:3)

**River** (Exodus 7:18)

**Spices** (Exodus 37:29)

**Vines** (Song of Solomon 2:13)

**Wounds** (Psalm 38:5)

# WORD SEARCH

```
S H O L Y S D N U O W N S A T
T C L E G Y P T E L E L I G E
S B A C K R S E K A R D N A M
C P R M Q U I D E T W I L R T
E D I A P D F E R D R F U M S
L T B C U S R A I E I N T E O
T F N I E N C D F A V M Y N R
T E G E Y S P F T D E W O T U
A N N A M D O I W F R F A S E
B G R O F T F S M L A N I D R
I N C E N S N H G I R M S T M
V W O R U D E I D E F L S E Y
M Y U S E O L A O S R B A U R
N B A T T E V I N E S O C L R
C O N E S N E C N I Q U I N H
```

# OVERCOME EVIL WITH GOOD

If it be **possible**, as much as **lieth** in you, **live peaceably** with <u>all men</u>. Dearly **beloved**, **avenge** not yourselves, but rather give place unto **wrath**: for it is **written**, **Vengeance** is **mine**; I will **repay**, saith the **Lord**. Therefore if thine **enemy hunger**, **feed** him; if he **thirst**, give him **drink**: for in so doing thou shalt **heap coals** of **fire** on his **head**. Be not **overcome** of **evil**, but overcome evil with **good**.

ROMANS 12:18–21

# WORD SEARCH

```
P O S E N E M Y K Y T E I L A
C O A L S L I V D O O G P V V
B E L B O H T A R W H T E T E
A W R I T T E N I F E N I M P
V H H S C O A P I W G H O A R
E E E S N D M R R E R D E D O
N A A O E S E I O O G H M T L
G R D P E A C E A B L Y O S A
D H E E P E A C F V E F C R L
R E V P V E D R I N K E R I L
O I O H A G N E E V D E E H M
L D L E R Y O G M I N T V T E
A V E N G E A N C E H G O H N
D R B L I V E U H U N G D O E
O V E R C I E H V C X T A R W
```

# ADAM AND EVE ARE CAST OUT OF THE GARDEN

Unto the woman he said, I will greatly **multiply** thy **sorrow** and thy **conception**; in sorrow thou shalt bring forth children; and thy desire shall be to thy **husband**, and he shall **rule** over thee. And unto **Adam** he said, Because thou hast **hearkened** unto the voice of thy wife, and hast __eaten of the tree__, of which I commanded thee, **saying**, Thou shalt not eat of it: **cursed** is the ground for thy sake; in sorrow shalt thou eat of it all the days of thy life; **thorns** also and **thistles** shall it bring forth to thee; and thou shalt eat the **herb** of the field; in the **sweat** of thy face shalt thou eat bread, till thou return unto the ground; for out of it wast thou taken: for __dust thou art__, and unto dust shalt thou **return**. And Adam called his wife's name **Eve**; because she was the **mother** of all living. Unto Adam also and to his wife did the LORD God make **coats** of **skins**, and **clothed** them. And the __LORD **God**__ said, Behold, the man is become as one of us, to know __good and evil__: and now, lest he put forth his hand, and take also of the __tree of life__, and eat, and live for ever: therefore the LORD God sent him forth from the garden of **Eden**, to till the ground from whence he was taken. So he drove out the man; and he placed at the **east** of the garden of Eden **Cherubims**, and a **flaming** sword which turned every way, to **keep** the way of the tree of life.

GENESIS 3:16–24

# WORD SEARCH

```
G S E L T S I H T M S E L U R
H O O D P E E K A I N A G T I
O L O R D G O D E C I T N R D
U W D D R E A V T O K E I E E
F A T N A O E X A N S N Y E H
S S R H A N W C E C Y O A O T
M D A F O B D O W E L F S F O
I E U L R R S E S P P T A L L
B N O A E T N U V T I H N I C
U E H M H Y C S H I T E R F E
R K T I T J U O X O L T U E K
E R T N O V R Z A N U R T N U
H A S G M E S Y I T M E E E O
C E U S B R E H X G S E R D N
Y H D I V A D F O S T S A E M
```

# FORGIVE

In this puzzle, can you find the word **_forgive_** 24 different times? It may help to make a tally mark in the space below each time you find one.

*For if ye forgive men their trespasses, your heavenly Father will also forgive you.*

MATTHEW 6:14

# WORD SEARCH

```
F G E F E E G I E O E I V O E
O I V I O G R V R V V F R G V
R V I V F R I F I F I O G F I
G E G F O G G G O V G R I O G
I O R V R F R I E G R G V F R
V F O O I O G V V I O I E O O
E O F G F R I G O E F V F R F
E R E V I G R O F V I E O G R
V G F G R I E I O G E F R I E
I I G O F V R V R I V O G V V
G V F V I E I O I R I R I E I
R E V G R V F R O G G G V O G
O I R F O R G I V E R V E V R
F O R G I V E F G O O O G R O
F I E V I G R O F I F V F O F
```

## KEEP GOING

And **David** said to **Solomon** his **son**, <u>**Be strong**</u> and of good **courage**, and do it: <u>**fear not**</u>, nor be **dismayed**: for the Lord God, even my God, will be with thee; he will not **fail** thee, nor **forsake** thee, until thou hast **finished** all the work for the **service** of the **house** of the Lord. And, **behold**, the **courses** of the **priests** and the **Levites**, even they shall be with thee for all the service of the house of God: and there shall be with thee for all **manner** of **workmanship** every **willing skilful** man, for any manner of service: also the princes and all the **people** will be **wholly** at thy **commandment**.

1 Chronicles 28:20–21

# WORD SEARCH

```
P C O U R S E S O L P M O E N
A H F E P E K A S R O F L S Y
K O D I V A D Y I W E N T U N
C R I B E Q U E L A M D R O L
G O S L A C S O R L A P S H E
N E M O K T I N G F O I L W V
I S A M S L O V M B S H A H I
L O Y J A T S P R G O S W E T
L R E R E N N A M E M N G N E
I C D T A M D L O H S A E L S
W A P S O L O M O N R M L I C
F I N I S H E D E U A K P A G
V H E B E S T R O N G R O F R
S K I L F U L C Q U T O E W O
O D L O H E B E M O N W P J U
```

# A BRILLIANT DISGUISE?

So the king of Israel and **Jehoshaphat** the king of Judah went up to **Ramothgilead**. And the king of Israel said unto Jehoshaphat, I will **disguise** myself, and enter into the battle; but put thou on thy **robes**. And the king of Israel disguised himself, and went into the battle. But the <u>**king of Syria commanded**</u> his thirty and two **captains** that had rule over his **chariots**, saying, **Fight** neither with small nor great, save only with the king of Israel. And it came to pass, when the captains of the chariots saw Jehoshaphat, that they said, Surely it is the king of Israel. And they turned aside to fight against him: and Jehoshaphat cried out. And it came to pass, when the captains of the chariots perceived that it was not the king of Israel, that they turned back from **pursuing** him. And a <u>**certain man**</u> <u>**drew a bow**</u> at a **venture**, and smote the king of Israel between the **joints** of the harness: wherefore he said unto the **driver** of his chariot, Turn thine hand, and carry me out of the host; for I am **wounded**. And the **battle** increased that day: and the king was stayed up in his chariot against the Syrians, and died at even: and the blood ran out of the wound into the midst of the chariot. And there went a proclamation throughout the **host** about the going down of the sun, saying, Every man to his city, and every man to his own country. So the king died, and was brought to **Samaria**; and they buried the king in Samaria. And one washed the chariot in the pool of Samaria; and the

# WORD SEARCH

```
X O A I R Y S F O G N I K J S
D O E R O D R E W A B O W G L
C R Z D A I R A M A S Y O T K
V B I X Z N F N R S M D U B P
E L A V T I I L U T A A N S U
S O I T E A G Y O O R E D U R
I O P V T R H N M I U L E C S
U D S R I L T P R R A I D O U
G R E M O M E Q A A L G P M I
S C O A T Y T S O H T H U M N
I W D B L L A I N C S T P A G
D R O L E H T F O D R O W N F
B Q U I P S T N I O J M H D H
M S N I A T P A C L P A E E G
X H O L L Y V E N T U R E D J
```

**dogs** licked up his **blood**; and they washed his **armour**; according unto the **word of the Lord** which he spake.

1 Kings 22:29–38

# MUTUAL FAITH

For God is my **witness**, whom I **serve** with my **spirit** in the **gospel** of his **Son**, that <u>without ceasing</u> I make **mention** of you **always** in my **prayers**; making **request**, if by any means now at **length** I might have a **prosperous journey** by the **will** of **God** to come unto you. For I long to see you, that I may **impart** unto you some **spiritual gift**, to the **end** ye may be **established**; that is, that I may be **comforted together** with you by the **mutual faith** both of <u>you and me</u>.

ROMANS 1:9–12

# WORD SEARCH

```
S  W  I  T  N  E  S  R  E  Y  A  R  P  S  T
Y  T  I  R  I  P  S  Q  I  R  I  P  S  E  O
A  W  I  T  N  E  S  S  G  I  F  L  O  R  G
W  I  M  S  H  Y  G  E  I  M  P  A  R  T  E
L  M  O  S  Y  O  Y  I  A  E  C  U  E  M  T
A  N  D  U  D  O  U  I  F  Y  I  T  Q  U  H
F  P  S  O  O  G  U  T  P  T  O  I  U  T  E
A  S  E  R  V  E  G  A  C  R  P  R  E  U  R
I  H  T  E  N  O  I  T  N  E  M  I  S  A  L
T  T  O  P  W  I  L  L  O  D  A  P  T  Q  E
H  G  G  S  O  L  A  U  T  U  M  S  O  R  P
U  N  E  O  Y  E  N  R  U  O  J  E  I  F  S
D  E  T  R  O  F  M  O  C  A  N  O  J  N  O
H  L  H  P  E  U  Q  E  R  D  U  I  O  Y  G
I  M  D  E  H  S  I  L  B  A  T  S  E  E  S
```

I will **praise** thee with <u>**my whole heart**</u>: before the gods will I sing praise unto thee. I will **worship** toward thy <u>**holy temple**</u>, and praise thy name for thy **lovingkindness** and for thy **truth**: for thou hast **magnified** thy word **above** all thy **name**. In the day when I cried thou **answeredst** me, and strengthenedst me with strength in my soul. <u>**All the kings**</u> of the earth shall praise thee, O Lᴏʀᴅ, **when** they hear the **words** of thy **mouth**. Yea, they shall sing in the ways of the Lᴏʀᴅ: for **great** is the glory of the Lᴏʀᴅ. **Though** the Lᴏʀᴅ be high, yet hath he **respect** unto the **lowly**: but the **proud** he knoweth **afar** off. Though I walk in the **midst of trouble**, thou wilt **revive** me: thou shalt **stretch** forth thine hand against the **wrath** of mine enemies, and thy <u>**right hand**</u> shall save me. The Lᴏʀᴅ will **perfect** that which concerneth me: thy mercy, O Lᴏʀᴅ, **endureth** for ever: forsake not the works of **thine** own hands.

# WORD SEARCH

```
Y H T E R U D N E H T U O M S
S A H C T E R T S E X A U Y H
H T U R T A H P S D H L S W T
E S B T E L P M E T Y L O H A
L D U D U O R P N H A T M O R
B E N Z E M A N D O F H A L W
U R V A A R I K N U A E G E P
O E X O H G S M I G R K N H E
R W J E B T E L K H T I I E R
T S D I M A H C G A A N F A F
F N T H I N E G N C E G I R E
R A L W O R S H I P R S E T C
O I K S H E Q U V R G V D O T
T C E P S E R W O R D S E H S
E V I V E R N Y L U Y L W O L
```

# THE HEART OF THE MATTER

Ye have **heard** that it was said of them of **old** time, Thou shalt not kill; and whosoever shall kill shall be in **danger** of the **judgment**: But I say unto you, That whosoever is **angry** with his **brother <u>without a cause</u>** shall be in danger of the judgment: and whosoever shall say to his brother, **Raca**, shall be in danger of the **council**: but whosoever shall say, Thou fool, shall be in danger of <u>**hell fire**</u>. Therefore if thou bring thy **gift** to the altar, and there rememberest that thy brother hath ought **against** thee; **leave** there thy gift before the **altar**, and go thy way; first <u>**be reconciled**</u> to thy brother, and then come and **offer** thy gift. Agree with thine **adversary** quickly, whiles thou art in the way with him; lest at any time the adversary **deliver** thee to the judge, and the judge deliver thee to the **officer**, and thou be cast into **prison**. Verily I say unto thee, Thou shalt by <u>**no means**</u> come out thence, till thou hast paid the uttermost farthing.

MATTHEW 5:21–26

# WORD SEARCH

```
W I L D A B E S T N O S I R P
Q I U L T G D H D Z X L C E V
P V T U A E B Q E U G K D B K
U A L H L R U K L L T S X M J
R I K I O J O M I G L A O T V
R N V T I U H Z C I N F B M S
E E H M F D T X N P F A I E N
R E A P T G Y A O I O D V R A
R Y O X A M O V C P C V G E E
E L P H C E J E E A O E H G M
F I E E R N R B R Y U R F N O
F N B A Q T D J E R N S D A N
O D C R V K F L B G C A E D E
A A Y D P E E I W N I R S C M
W P U T S N I A G A L Y W B R
```

# JESUS RAISES A WIDOW'S SON

And it came to pass the **day** after, that he went into a **city** called **Nain**; and many of his **disciples** went with him, and much **people**. Now when he came nigh to the **gate** of the city, behold, there was a <u>**dead man**</u> carried out, the only **son** of his **mother**, and she was a **widow**: and much people of the city was with her. And when the **Lord** saw her, he had **compassion** on her, and said unto her, <u>**Weep not**</u>. And he came and touched the **bier**: and they that bare him stood still. And he said, Young man, I say unto thee, **Arise**. And he that was dead **sat** up, and began to **speak**. And he **delivered** him to his mother. And there came a **fear** on all: and they **glorified** God, saying, That a great **prophet** is risen up among us; and, That **God** hath visited his people. And this **rumour** of him went forth throughout all **Judaea**, and throughout all the **region** round about.

LUKE 7:11–17

# WORD SEARCH

```
B T N V U J R N V A E W N F P
C O U B T U D E R E V I L E D
S N Z D C D O W R E H T O M N
E P D H Q A G N K J Y P T A S
L E E F U E D V K F L G I M D
P E I B N A F A F E O N N I E
I W F F O E E A D S R N P U A
C P I M I P A M G E D R Y T D
S O R O S V R V G D O V Q R M
I U O V S K L I G P W W B U A
D E L D A N O J H N G I N F N
R H G D P N E E F W E U D S C
G V H H M P T U O R L Y G O F
V S F J O U A R I S E Y A M W
W Y T I C I G R U O M U R D O
```

# PAUL AND SILAS

And at **midnight Paul** and **Silas prayed**, and **sang praises** unto **God**: and the **prisoners** heard them. And suddenly there was a <u>**great earthquake**</u>, so that the **foundations** of the prison were **shaken**: and immediately all the **doors** were **opened**, and every one's **bands** were **loosed**. And the **keeper** of the prison **awaking** out of his **sleep**, and seeing the prison doors open, he **drew** out his **sword**, and would have killed himself, supposing that the prisoners had been **fled**. But Paul cried with a loud **voice**, saying, Do **thyself** <u>**no harm**</u>: for we are all **here**.

ACTS 16:25–28

# WORD SEARCH

```
V O I B S H P E E L S E R G L
S I L A O A W A K I N G N G U
T K E N P E M O A W M N A B A
J H Q D O P R G U D E Y A R P
E R G S P Y A E Q U R E H F L
E A R I E A H G H P O E S O F
L S S I N S O H T L S R W U R
S D R L E D N W R A B O O N E
S E E E D P I S A N G O R D P
E E P S N S W M E E O D D A E
S K S R O O D A T K R E H T E
I I N O H O S O A A U O F I K
A F L E D L L I E H E C I O V
R G O A I A R P R S L I S N O
P T H Y S E L F G P D I M S N
```

*ninety-six* **96**

# WAIT QUIETLY BEFORE GOD

**Truly** my **soul waiteth** upon God: from him cometh my **salvation**. He only is **my rock** and my salvation; he is my **defence**; I shall not be greatly **moved**. How long will ye **imagine mischief** against a **man**? ye shall be slain all of you: as a **bowing wall** shall ye be, and as a **tottering** fence. They only **consult** to cast him down from his **excellency**: they **delight** in **lies**: they **bless** with their **mouth**, but they **curse** inwardly. **Selah**. My soul, wait thou only **upon God**; for my **expectation** is from him. He only is my rock and my salvation: he is my defence; I shall not be moved.

Psalm 62:1–6

# WORD SEARCH

```
B L O M C L M I S C H I E F R
G N I R E T T O T B U N T D S
H T E T I A W H V O A G R E I
C A R M E C G L C E L S I F T
M V O U W I N D S U D L N E L
O L T T L G U P O N G O D N U
U L V E A Y Q S V B I E M C S
T A D C H I E F L T L O A E N
H W B L E N I G A M I C N S O
Z G H T H U L T R O N I P R C
E N M Y R O C K F L A S H U P
K I J I V E X C E L L E N C Y
E W O N P A L N S I N G H A L
P O G X N O I T A V L A S B R
H B E M A S S E L B S E L A H
```

# FIVE CROSSES #4

In this puzzle, you will find five-letter words that are commonly found in the Bible. Your search will be aided by the fact that each word has a partner word that crosses its center, forming either an "x" or a "+" shape.

| | |
|---|---|
| **Alive** | **Pearl** |
| **Blood** | **Plant** |
| **Brick** | **Price** |
| **Chose** | **Raise** |
| **Drunk** | **Renew** |
| **Faint** | **Saint** |
| **Flame** | **Shout** |
| **Grace** | **Snare** |
| **Grain** | **Songs** |
| **Grave** | **Souls** |
| **Hands** | **Spear** |
| **Hides** | **Stone** |
| **House** | **Sweet** |
| **Judge** | **Unity** |
| **Manna** | **White** |
| **Mount** | **Wrath** |

# WORD SEARCH

```
B G W N T F K I H L A Q K I G
A U R S L J A W E A B S W H O
M H U A E R M R E N O V T J U
T P M J I V A H A N D S N R M
R E K R U N I E G A E C I R P
L A C N S D B S P M G R A E V
W H I T E O G U L H O T S N B
I T R S T O N E N I S U A M S
Y H B W E L P E A B O W N P I
U L I M T B T L C H R B E T D
D N E P S U G H S A T A F E A
G R S L C J O R T N R N Y L T
A B U W G S R H A E M G I E S
L O K N E T U L S V B V U A Z
S I M S K H P V I N E K L G F
```

# JUST DROP IT

At that time Jesus answered and said, I thank thee, **O Father**, Lord of **heaven and earth**, because thou hast **hid** these things from the **wise** and **prudent**, and hast **revealed** them unto **babes**. Even so, Father: for so it **seemed good** in thy sight. **All things** are **delivered** unto me of my Father: and no man knoweth the Son, but the Father; neither knoweth any man the Father, save the Son, and he to whomsoever the Son will reveal him. **Come** unto me, all ye that **labour** and are **heavy laden**, and I will give you **rest**. Take my **yoke** upon you, and **learn** of me; for I am meek and **lowly in heart**: and ye shall **find rest** unto your **souls**. For my yoke is **easy**, and my **burden** is **light**.

MATTHEW 11:25–30

# WORD SEARCH

```
Q  J  P  R  U  D  E  N  T  Q  R  T  Q  U  R
U  E  Y  S  A  E  G  E  P  M  E  S  A  H  E
A  O  T  B  U  L  O  D  A  J  H  E  T  E  V
C  O  J  R  S  I  P  R  I  G  T  R  C  A  E
K  Z  V  L  A  V  R  U  P  H  A  D  W  V  A
C  D  U  Q  X  E  M  B  A  E  F  N  P  Y  L
T  O  C  X  S  R  H  U  D  L  O  I  T  L  E
S  O  M  T  V  E  T  N  D  H  M  F  S  A  D
U  G  B  E  N  D  A  Y  I  G  A  T  U  D  P
N  D  S  Y  L  N  Y  Z  H  Y  X  O  R  E  R
N  E  E  L  E  O  H  U  O  J  L  K  T  N  U
Y  M  B  V  W  F  M  K  W  E  I  W  R  T  O
L  E  A  R  N  I  E  X  P  O  G  I  O  U  B
M  E  B  H  G  A  S  G  N  I  H  T  L  L  A
H  S  W  O  I  P  L  E  F  D  T  B  V  C  L
```

# MY SHEEP

**Jesus** answered them, I told you, and ye **believed** not: the **works** that I do in my **Father's name**, they **bear witness** of me. But ye **believe not**, because ye are not of my **sheep**, as I said unto you. My sheep **hear** my **voice**, and I **know** them, and they **follow** me: and I give unto them **eternal life**; and they shall **never perish**, neither shall any man **pluck** them out of my **hand**. **My Father**, which gave them me, is **greater** than all; and no man is able to pluck them out of my Father's hand.

JOHN 10:25–29

# WORD SEARCH

```
J R A E B K A N R E T E H I W
E W I N T B L I F R A E O F W
S F A T H E R S K N A H S O L
U M I E D L F Y M R L P R L O
E H E A W I T N E S S K E L F
G R E T A E R G A T S D I O R
J S H E U V O I C E E F R W E
P E R P L E B R J E E R O W E
L T S L P D S H E E P O N W H
U W O U F A T H E H A N D A S
C L I C S W I T N E T A E B L
W O N K N A M U E T E A T E R
N E V E R P E R I S H S F Y O
E P L T O N E V E I L E B Y W
N B E A B E L I E V U H F Y M
```

# Answer Key

## 1—The Coming of the Lord

## 2—Baptize

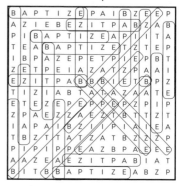

## 3—Ask and Believe

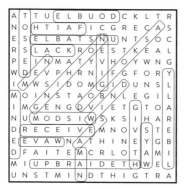

## 4—Adjectives for God

## 5—Promise Through Faith

## 6—Couples Cross

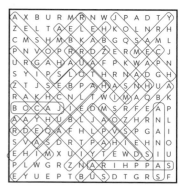

Sarah, Eve, Sapphira, Priscilla, Ruth, Bathsheba,
Gomer, Rebekah, Rachel, Mary, Zipporah, Elisabeth

## 7—A Doer of the Word

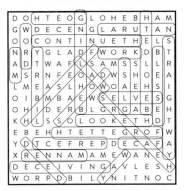

## 8—God Meant It for Good

Who was the father of Joseph and his eleven fearful brothers? Jacob (Genesis 35:22–26)

## 9—Nehemiah Prays for Israel

## 10—Eli's Fall

## 11—Lineage of Noah

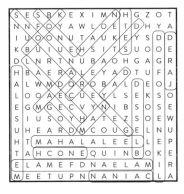

## 12—Obey Your Masters

## 13—A Crooked Choice

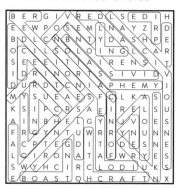

## 14—Grace Be unto You

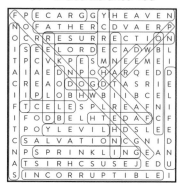

## 15—The Origins of King Saul

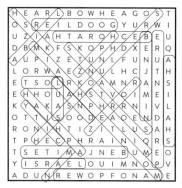

## 16—Places of Biblical Wars and Battles

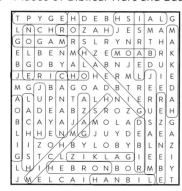

## 17— Grace and Peace Be Multiplied

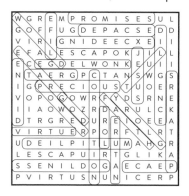

## 18— Three-Syllable Names in the Bible

## 19—God of. . . (Old Testament)

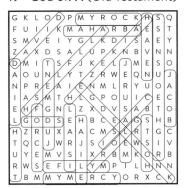

## 20—Above All Things

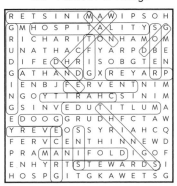

## 21— Items Found in Biblical Dreams

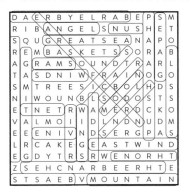

## 22—The Lord Upholds My Life

## 23—Psalm 115:1–18

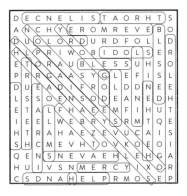

## 24—Count on Children

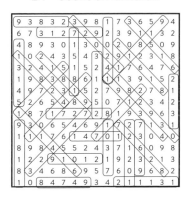

## 25— Pharoah's Daughter Finds Moses

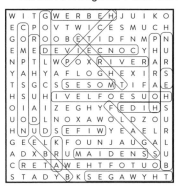

## 26—A Changed Life

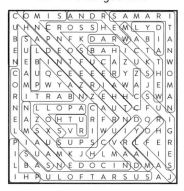

## 27—Lineage of Jesus

## 28—Paul in Corinth (Acts 18)

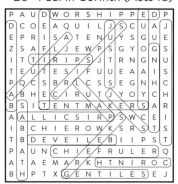

## 29—Daniel Is Promoted

## 30—Courageous Midwives

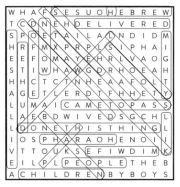

What plan did Pharaoh hatch after the midwives chose no[t] to kill the baby boys? *"Pharaoh charged all his people, sayi[ng,] Every son that is born ye shall cast into the river, and ever[y] daughter ye shall save alive"* (Exodus 1:22).

## 31—Psalm 4:1–8

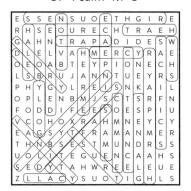

## 32— Bible Men with Multiple Mates

## 33—Peter's Sermon

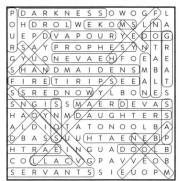

## 34— Two-Syllable Names in the Bible

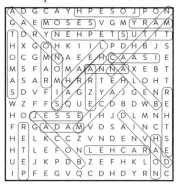

## 35—Noah Leaves the Ark

## 36—Five Crosses #1

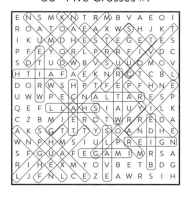

## 37—Joshua Renews the Covenant

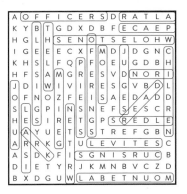

## 38— Things Found in the Land of Israel

## 39—The Hope in You

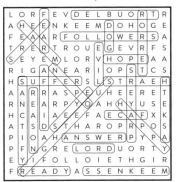

## 40—Prayer Changes Things

## 41—Moses Returns to Egypt

## 42—Pool of Siloam (John 9)

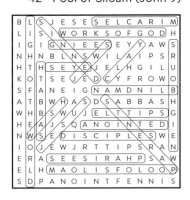

## 43—Growing Up

## 44—God of. . . (New Testament)

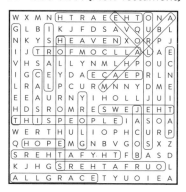

## 45—A Prayer for Israel

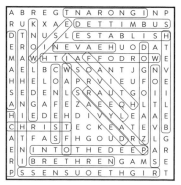

## 46—King Me

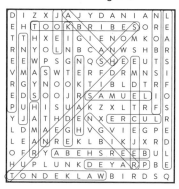

## 47—By Him

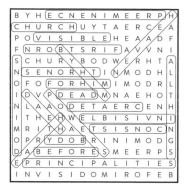

## 48— Shhh. . . We're Building the Temple

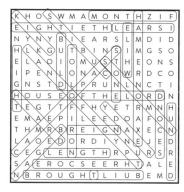

How many years did King Solomon spend
constructing the temple of the Lord in
Jerusalem? Seven (1 Kings 6:38)

## 49—Jonah Defies God

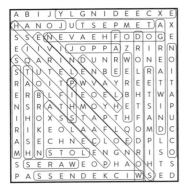

## 50—Noah's Descendants

## 51—Faith

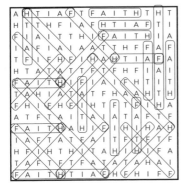

## 52—He Gave Gifts

## 53—A New Thing

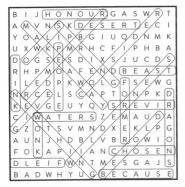

## 54—The Throne in Heaven

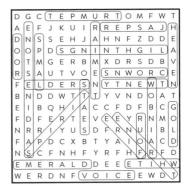

## 55—How Dry I Am

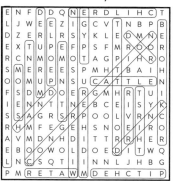

## 56—God Shall Be with You

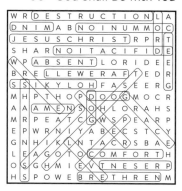

## 57—Not Ashamed

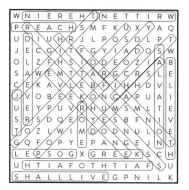

## 58—Israel Called to Repentance

## 59—Psalm 21:1-13

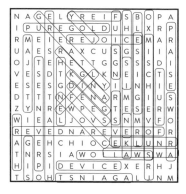

## 60—Count on Eternal Life

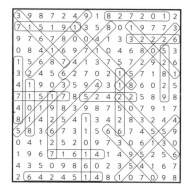

## 61—Widow of Nain (Luke 7:11–17)

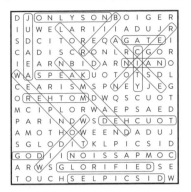

## 62—The Tree of Life

## 63—God Is. . . (Part 1)

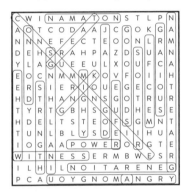

## 64— Elijah Stays with a Widow Woman

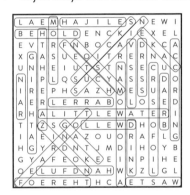

## 65—Five Crosses #2

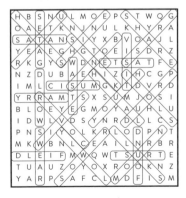

## 66—As He Purposeth

## 67—Live Right

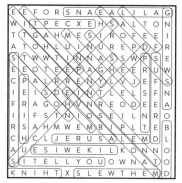

## 68—A Bend in the River

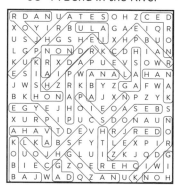

## 69—From the Headlines of the *Jerusalem News*

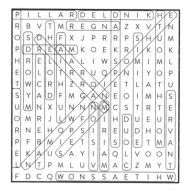

For what other feature was the village of Siloam well known? A pool (John 9:7)

## 70—Walk by Faith

## 71—Snow White

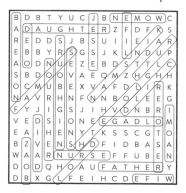

## 72—Ruth and Boaz Marry

## 73—God Is. . . (Part 2)

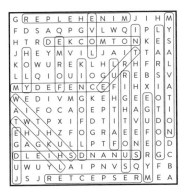

## 74—Number the Stars

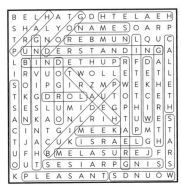

## 75—Where Wast Thou?

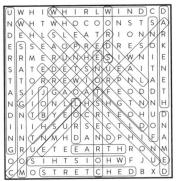

Which two constellations are mentioned in this chapter of Job? Pleiades and Orion (Job 38:31)

## 76—Esther Reveals Haman's Plot

## 77—Count on Hospitality

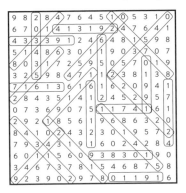

## 78— Traditions and Commandments

## 79—Oh, Promise Me

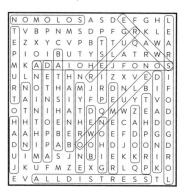

## 80—The Death of King David

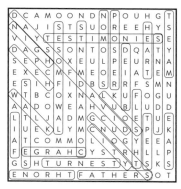

## 81— Announcement to Mary
### (Luke 1:26–38)

## 82—The Purpose of Parables

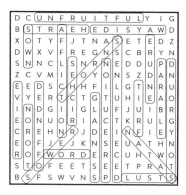

## 83—Every Thought Captive

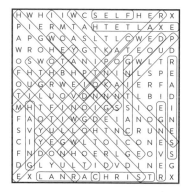

## 84—Five Crosses #3

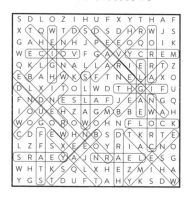

Which expert apostle wrote down this powerful bit of instruction for godly living? Paul (2 Corinthians 1:1)

## 85—Smells in the Bible

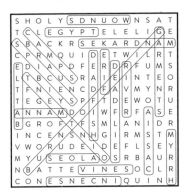

## 86—Overcome Evil with Good

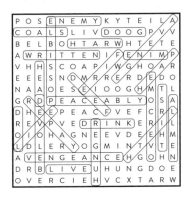

## 87— Adam and Eve Are Cast Out of the Garden

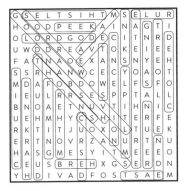

## 88—Forgive

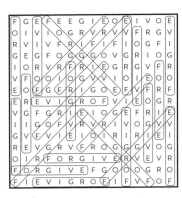

## 89—Keep Going

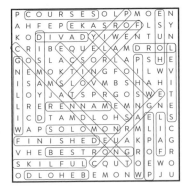

## 90—A Brilliant Disguise?

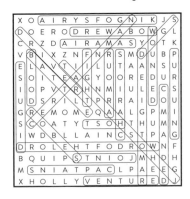

## 91—Mutual Faith

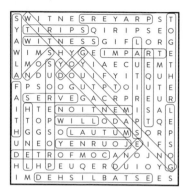

## 92—Psalm 138:1–8

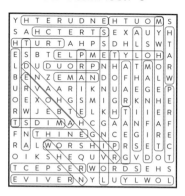

## 93—The Heart of the Matter

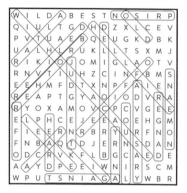

## 94—Jesus Raises a Widow's Son

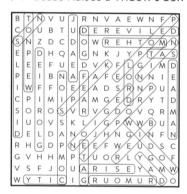

## 95—Paul and Silas

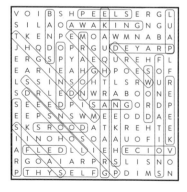

## 96—Wait Quietly Before God

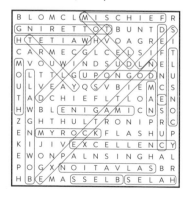

### 97—Five Crosses #4

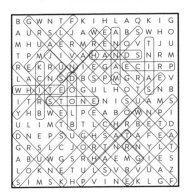

### 98—Just Drop It

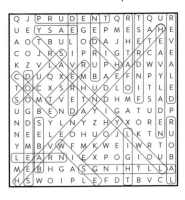

### 99—My Sheep

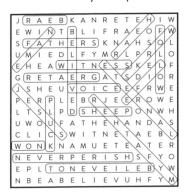

## *Looking for more fun?*

# FUN BIBLE CROSSWORDS

Paperback / 978-1-64352-092-6 / $12.99

Bible puzzles are a great way to pass time while learning scripture—and here's a collection of 99 crosswords sure to satisfy.

With clues drawn from the breadth of scripture, these themed puzzles will challenge and expand your knowledge of the Good Book.

Inside, you'll find puzzles on

- Angels
- Christmas
- Favorite Bible Stories
- the Gospel
- Noah's Ark
- Prophets and Prophecies
- the Proverbs
- and much, much more

Based on the King James and New King James versions of scripture, some clues and answers are drawn from other fields of study for added variety.

If you enjoy Bible crosswords (and who doesn't?), you'll love *Fun Bible Crosswords*!